TEXAS TEST PREP

STAAR Practice Test Book

STAAR Mathematics

Grade 5

ISBN 978-1725164680

TEST MASTER PRESS

www.testmasterpress.com

CONTENTS

INTRODUCTION
For Parents, Teachers, and Tutors

About the STAAR Assessments and the Revised TEKS Skills

Students in Texas will be assessed each year by taking a set of tests known as the State of Texas Assessments of Academic Readiness, or STAAR. Beginning with the 2014-2015 school year, the assessments will cover the skills listed in the revised TEKS for mathematics. The questions in this book cover all the skills in the revised TEKS and will prepare students for the STAAR assessments.

About the Practice Tests

This practice test book contains three complete STAAR Mathematics tests. Each test contains 60 questions. This is slightly more than the actual tests that contain 50 questions. The extra questions will ensure that students have practice with all the skills assessed on the actual state test.

Types of Questions

The majority of the test is made up of multiple-choice questions. Students can answer the questions by filling in the circle of their answer choice in the test book. Students can also answer the questions by filling in the circles on the answer sheet in the back of the book. The test also contains several gridded-response questions where students write their answers in a grid.

Timing the Test

Students are given 4 hours to complete the actual STAAR mathematics test. This can be divided into two or more sessions, but all sessions are always completed on the same day. The practice tests in this book have been divided into two sessions. To account for the extra questions, students should be able to complete each session in 2.5 hours. You can use this time limit, or you can choose not to time the test.

Calculators and Tools

Students should be provided with a ruler to use on both sessions of the test. Students are not allowed to use a calculator on any session of the STAAR tests, and so should complete all the practice tests without the use of a calculator.

STAAR Mathematics

Grade 5

Practice Test 1

Session 1

Directions

Read each question carefully. For a multiple-choice question, determine the best answer to the question from the four answer choices provided.

For a griddable question, determine the best answer. Write your answer at the top of the grid. Then shade the grid to show your answer.

You may use a ruler to help you answer questions. You may also use the information on the Reference Sheet at the back of this book. You may not use a calculator on this test.

1   Troy recorded the number of sales he made each month.

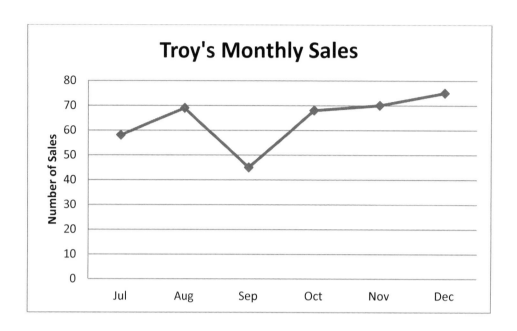

Between which two months did Troy's sales increase the most?

Ⓐ   July to August

Ⓑ   August to September

Ⓒ   September to October

Ⓓ   November to December

2   A school has 7 school buses. Each bus can seat 48 students. A total of 303 students get on the buses to go to a school camp. How many empty seats would there be on the buses? Record your answer and fill in the bubbles on the grid. Be sure to use the correct place value.

			.		
⓪	⓪	⓪		⓪	⓪
①	①	①		①	①
②	②	②		②	②
③	③	③		③	③
④	④	④		④	④
⑤	⑤	⑤		⑤	⑤
⑥	⑥	⑥		⑥	⑥
⑦	⑦	⑦		⑦	⑦
⑧	⑧	⑧		⑧	⑧
⑨	⑨	⑨		⑨	⑨

3   A fraction representing $\frac{6}{8}$ is shown below.

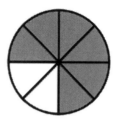

What is the value of $\frac{6}{8} \div 3$?

Ⓐ $\frac{1}{8}$

Ⓑ $\frac{3}{8}$

Ⓒ $\frac{1}{4}$

Ⓓ $\frac{3}{4}$

4   A jug of milk contains 4 pints of milk. Michael pours 1 cup of milk from the jug. How much milk is left in the jug?

Ⓐ   3 cups

Ⓑ   6 cups

Ⓒ   7 cups

Ⓓ   8 cups

5   A square garden has side lengths of 4.5 feet. What is the area of the garden? You can use the diagram below to help find the answer.

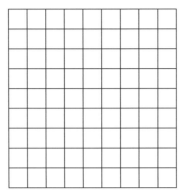

Each square is 0.5 foot × 0.5 foot.
Each square has an area of 0.25 square feet.

Ⓐ   16.25 square feet

Ⓑ   20.25 square feet

Ⓒ   40.5 square feet

Ⓓ   182.25 square feet

6   A box contains 24 cans of soups. Gerald orders 8 boxes of soup for his store. He is charged $0.50 for each can of soup. What is the total cost of the soup Gerald ordered?

Ⓐ $12

Ⓑ $64

Ⓒ $96

Ⓓ $384

7   Which ordered pair represents a point located inside both rectangles?

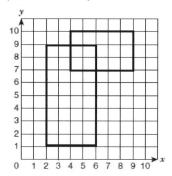

Ⓐ   (8, 6)

Ⓑ   (5, 8)

Ⓒ   (4, 10)

Ⓓ   (7, 9)

8   How is the numeral 35.012 written in words?

Ⓐ   Thirty-five thousand and twelve

Ⓑ   Thirty-five and twelve thousandths

Ⓒ   Thirty-five and twelve hundredths

Ⓓ   Thirty-five and twelve

9   Which point represents the location of the ordered pair $(1\frac{1}{4}, 2\frac{1}{2})$?

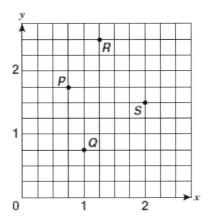

Ⓐ   Point *P*

Ⓑ   Point *Q*

Ⓒ   Point *R*

Ⓓ   Point *S*

10   Which term describes all the shapes shown below?

Ⓐ   Parallelogram

Ⓑ   Rectangle

Ⓒ   Rhombus

Ⓓ   Square

11 Mitch ran 2.6 miles on Monday and 1.8 miles on Tuesday. How many miles less did Mitch run on Tuesday?

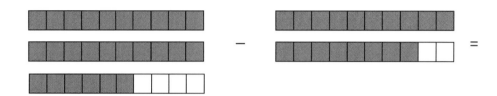

Record your answer and fill in the bubbles on the grid. Be sure to use the correct place value.

12 Victor rode 3.65 kilometers to his friend's house. How many meters did Victor ride?

Ⓐ   365 meters

Ⓑ   3,650 meters

Ⓒ   36,500 meters

Ⓓ   365,000 meters

13 The table below shows the temperature recorded each hour from 9 a.m. to 2 p.m.

Time	Temperature (°C)
9 a.m.	8
10 a.m.	11
11 a.m.	13
12 noon	16
1 p.m.	17
2 p.m.	19

Steve wants to draw a graph to show how the temperature changed from 9 a.m. to 2 p.m. Which type of graph would Steve be best to use?

Ⓐ   Stem-and-leaf plot

Ⓑ   Scatterplot

Ⓒ   Pictograph

Ⓓ   Dot plot

14   The fine for having a DVD overdue is a basic fee of $4 plus an additional $2 for each day that the movie is overdue. Which equation can be used to find c, the cost in dollars of the fine for d days?

ⓐ $c = 2d + 4$

ⓑ $c = 4d + 2$

ⓒ $c = 2(d + 4)$

ⓓ $c = 4(d + 2)$

15   Leonard bought 12 tickets to a charity event. The total cost of the tickets was $216. The expression below can be used to find the cost of each ticket.

$$216 \div 12$$

Which of the following is equivalent to the above expression?

ⓐ $(240 \div 12) + (24 \div 12)$

ⓑ $(200 \div 10) + (16 \div 2)$

ⓒ $(216 \div 10) + (216 \div 2)$

ⓓ $(120 \div 12) + (96 \div 12)$

16   Which number is a composite number?

    Ⓐ   67

    Ⓑ   73

    Ⓒ   89

    Ⓓ   97

17   Wayne needs to add the fractions below.

$$\frac{1}{5}, \frac{5}{7}, \frac{9}{10}$$

Wayne first needs to determine the least common multiple of the denominators. What is the least common multiple of the denominators?

    Ⓐ   35

    Ⓑ   50

    Ⓒ   70

    Ⓓ   350

18   Which term describes the triangle below?

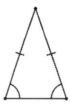

    Ⓐ   Isosceles

    Ⓑ   Scalene

    Ⓒ   Equilateral

    Ⓓ   Right

19   What is the value of $1\frac{2}{5} \div 2$? You can use the model below to help find the answer.

    Ⓐ $\frac{1}{6}$

    Ⓑ $\frac{2}{7}$

    Ⓒ $\frac{7}{10}$

    Ⓓ $1\frac{1}{5}$

20   The factor tree for the number 60 is shown below.

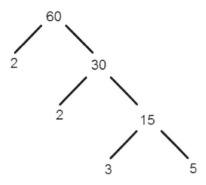

According to the factor tree, which statement is true?

Ⓐ   The number 30 is prime.

Ⓑ   The only prime factor of 60 is 2.

Ⓒ   The numbers 15 and 30 are prime factors of 60.

Ⓓ   The numbers 2, 3, and 5 are prime factors of 60.

21 The table below shows the total number of pounds of flour in different numbers of bags of flour.

Number of Bags	Number of Pounds
3	12
5	20
8	32
9	36

What is the relationship between the number of bags of flour and the number of pounds of flour?

Ⓐ   The number of pounds is 9 more than the number of bags.

Ⓑ   The number of pounds is 15 more than the number of bags.

Ⓒ   The number of pounds is 4 times the number of bags.

Ⓓ   The number of pounds is 6 times the number of bags.

22 Which statement is true about the product of $\frac{1}{3}$ and 6?

Ⓐ   The product is greater than 6.

Ⓑ   The product is less than $\frac{1}{3}$.

Ⓒ   The product is a value between the two factors.

Ⓓ   The product is a value equal to one of the factors.

23   The model below is made up of 1-centimeter cubes.

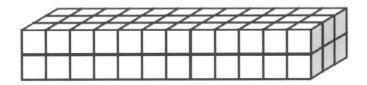

What is a correct way to find the volume of the model?

Ⓐ   12 cm x 6 cm

Ⓑ   2 cm x 6 cm x 12 cm

Ⓒ   2 cm x 3 cm x 12 cm

Ⓓ   12 cm x 12 cm

24   How many centimeters are equivalent to 400 millimeters?

Ⓐ   0.4 cm

Ⓑ   4 cm

Ⓒ   40 cm

Ⓓ   4000 cm

25 What is the value of the expression below?

$$(16 + 20) - 8 \div 4$$

Ⓐ   1

Ⓑ   7

Ⓒ   19

Ⓓ   34

26 A square poster has side lengths of 8 inches. What is the area of the poster?

Ⓐ   32 square inches

Ⓑ   36 square inches

Ⓒ   48 square inches

Ⓓ   64 square inches

27 Tom worked for 32 hours and earned $448. He earned the same rate per hour. How much does Tom earn per hour, in dollars? Record your answer and fill in the bubbles on the grid. Be sure to use the correct place value.

			.		
⓪	⓪	⓪		⓪	⓪
①	①	①		①	①
②	②	②		②	②
③	③	③		③	③
④	④	④		④	④
⑤	⑤	⑤		⑤	⑤
⑥	⑥	⑥		⑥	⑥
⑦	⑦	⑦		⑦	⑦
⑧	⑧	⑧		⑧	⑧
⑨	⑨	⑨		⑨	⑨

28   Joe made the graph below to show the locations of prizes he hid for a treasure hunt. Each star represents a treasure.

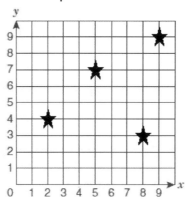

Samantha started searching at the origin. Which ordered pair represents the location of the treasure closest to Samantha?

Ⓐ   (2, 4)

Ⓑ   (5, 7)

Ⓒ   (8, 3)

Ⓓ   (9, 9)

29 Which of these should be placed in the overlapping section of the Venn diagram below?

rhombus   rectangle   square

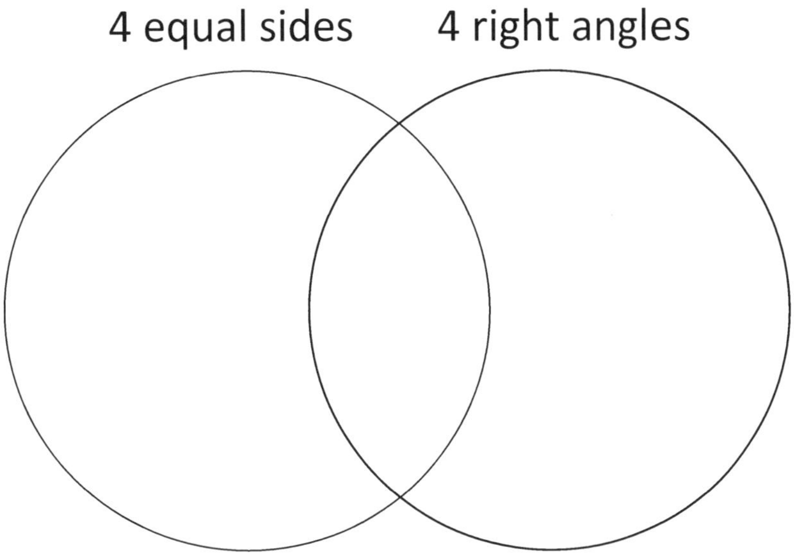

4 equal sides   4 right angles

Ⓐ   rhombus only

Ⓑ   square only

Ⓒ   rectangle and square

Ⓓ   square and rhombus

30   William surveyed students on how long it took them to travel to school each morning. The table shows the results.

Time	Number of Students
0 to 10 minutes	22
11 to 30 minutes	36
31 to 60 minutes	14
Over 60 minutes	3

Which type of graph would William be best to use to summarize the survey results?

Ⓐ   Bar graph

Ⓑ   Scatterplot

Ⓒ   Line graph

Ⓓ   Stem-and-leaf plot

END OF SESSION 1

STAAR Mathematics

Grade 5

Practice Test 1

Session 2

Directions

Read each question carefully. For a multiple-choice question, determine the best answer to the question from the four answer choices provided.

For a griddable question, determine the best answer. Write your answer at the top of the grid. Then shade the grid to show your answer.

You may use a ruler to help you answer questions. You may also use the information on the Reference Sheet at the back of this book. You may not use a calculator on this test.

---

31   To complete a calculation correctly, Mark moves the decimal place of 420.598 two places to the left.

$$420.598 \rightarrow 4.20598$$

Which of these describes the calculation completed?

Ⓐ   Dividing by 10

Ⓑ   Dividing by 100

Ⓒ   Multiplying by 10

Ⓓ   Multiplying by 100

32   If the numbers below were each rounded to the nearest tenth, which number would be rounded down?

Ⓐ   17.386

Ⓑ   23.758

Ⓒ   35.672

Ⓓ   54.127

33 A recipe for pancakes requires $2\frac{2}{3}$ cups of flour. Donna only has $1\frac{1}{2}$ cups of flour. How many more cups of flour does Donna need?

Ⓐ $\frac{1}{3}$ cup

Ⓑ $\frac{1}{6}$ cup

Ⓒ $1\frac{1}{3}$ cups

Ⓓ $1\frac{1}{6}$ cups

34 When Leo buys a kite, he is charged $18 plus a tax of 5.25%. What type of tax is Leo charged?

Ⓐ Income tax

Ⓑ Payroll tax

Ⓒ Sales tax

Ⓓ Property tax

35   The table below shows the total cost of hiring DVDs for different numbers of DVDs.

Number of DVDs	Total Cost
2	$6
5	$15
6	$18
8	$24

Which equation could be used to find the total cost, c, of hiring x DVDs?

Ⓐ $c = x + 4$

Ⓑ $c = 3x$

Ⓒ $c = x + 3$

Ⓓ $c = 8x$

36   Dave bought 4 packets of pies. Three packets had 12 pies each, and one packet had 10 pies. Which number sentence shows the total number of pies Dave bought?

Ⓐ   (3 x 12) x 10

Ⓑ   (3 + 12) x 10

Ⓒ   (3 x 12) + 10

Ⓓ   (3 + 12) + 10

37 Candice has a painting canvas that is 0.5 feet long and 0.5 feet wide. What is the area of the canvas? You can shade the diagram below to help find the area of the canvas.

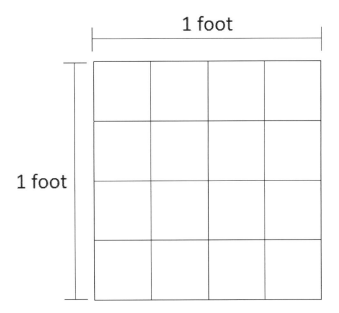

Ⓐ   0.05 square feet

Ⓑ   0.25 square feet

Ⓒ   0.5 square feet

Ⓓ   1 square feet

38   The grid below represents Dani's living room.

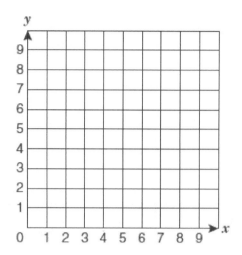

The television is located at the point (5, 4). A lamp is sitting 4 units to the right of the television and 3 units down from the television. Which ordered pair represents the location of the lamp?

Ⓐ   (0, 2)

Ⓑ   (1, 1)

Ⓒ   (8, 2)

Ⓓ   (9, 1)

39 The table below shows the number of households in four different suburbs.

Suburb	Number of Households
Wellington	135,682
Ashton	179,441
Ellis	120,597
Mayfield	191,822

How many more households does Mayfield have than Ashton?

Ⓐ   12,381

Ⓑ   12,481

Ⓒ   22,381

Ⓓ   22,481

40 A rectangular toy box has a length of 90 centimeters, a width of 30 centimeters, and a height of 50 centimeters. What is the volume of the toy box?

Ⓐ   4,500 cubic centimeters

Ⓑ   6,000 cubic centimeters

Ⓒ   81,000 cubic centimeters

Ⓓ   135,000 cubic centimeters

41   The table below shows the prices of items at a cake stall.

Item	Price
Small cake	$1.85
Muffin	$2.25
Cookie	$0.95

Sarah bought one small cake, one muffin, and one cookie. Which is the best estimate of the amount Sarah spent?

Ⓐ $3.00

Ⓑ $4.00

Ⓒ $5.00

Ⓓ $6.00

42   Lewis scored 0.15 of the points in a basketball game. How many of the team's 120 points did Lewis score?

Ⓐ   15

Ⓑ   18

Ⓒ   20

Ⓓ   35

43 Graham finds he is spending more than his budget. What are the two actions he could take to balance the budget?

Ⓐ Increase income or increase spending

Ⓑ Increase income or decrease spending

Ⓒ Decrease income or increase spending

Ⓓ Decrease income or decrease spending

44 Camille cooked a cake on high for $1\frac{1}{4}$ hours. She then cooked it for another $\frac{1}{2}$ hour on low. Which diagram represents how long she cooked the cake for in all?

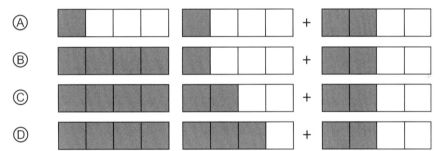

45   Which number makes the number sentence below true?

$$2 \div \square = 8$$

Ⓐ $\frac{1}{2}$

Ⓑ $\frac{1}{4}$

Ⓒ $\frac{1}{8}$

Ⓓ $\frac{1}{16}$

46   The table below shows the cost of hiring CDs, DVDs, and video games from a hire store.

Item	Cost per Week
CD	$2
DVD	$3
Video game	$4

Which expression represents the total cost of hiring c CDs and d DVDs for w weeks?

Ⓐ $2c + 3d + w$

Ⓑ $w(2c + 3d)$

Ⓒ $w(2c) + 3d$

Ⓓ $2c + 3d$

47   The wingspan of the butterfly is 67.2 millimeters.

What is the wingspan of the butterfly in centimeters? Record your answer and fill in the bubbles on the grid. Be sure to use the correct place value.

			.		
⓪	⓪	⓪		⓪	⓪
①	①	①		①	①
②	②	②		②	②
③	③	③		③	③
④	④	④		④	④
⑤	⑤	⑤		⑤	⑤
⑥	⑥	⑥		⑥	⑥
⑦	⑦	⑦		⑦	⑦
⑧	⑧	⑧		⑧	⑧
⑨	⑨	⑨		⑨	⑨

48   The model below was made with 1-unit cubes.

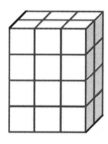

What is the volume of the model?

Ⓐ   16 cubic units

Ⓑ   24 cubic units

Ⓒ   26 cubic units

Ⓓ   36 cubic units

49   What is the value of the expression below?

$$28 + 4 \div 2 + (9 - 5)$$

Ⓐ   20

Ⓑ   30

Ⓒ   34

Ⓓ   44

50 The table shows the amount of rainfall for the first four days of May.

Date	1st	2nd	3rd	4th
Rainfall (cm)	4.59	4.43	4.50	4.61

Which day had the lowest rainfall?

Ⓐ 1st

Ⓑ 2nd

Ⓒ 3rd

Ⓓ 4th

51 Sam kept a record of the types of movies each customer in his store rented. Sam made the frequency table below to show the results.

Type of Movie	Number of Rentals
Action	┼┼┼┼ ┼┼┼┼ ‖
Comedy	┼┼┼┼ ┼┼┼┼ ‖‖
Drama	┼┼┼┼ ┼┼┼┼ ┼┼┼┼ │
Science fiction	┼┼┼┼ ‖│

What fraction of the movies rented were comedies?

Ⓐ $\frac{1}{4}$

Ⓑ $\frac{7}{50}$

Ⓒ $\frac{7}{25}$

Ⓓ $\frac{12}{43}$

52 The table shows the best times for running 100 meters of four students on the track team.

Student	Best Time (seconds)
Ramon	12.77
Ellis	12.63
Xavier	12.75
Colin	12.68

If each time is rounded to the nearest tenth, which student would have a best time of 12.7 seconds?

Ⓐ   Ramon

Ⓑ   Ellis

Ⓒ   Xavier

Ⓓ   Colin

53 Greg's volleyball team returns $\frac{4}{5}$ of the serves. How many serves out of 100 would the team expect to return?

Ⓐ   45

Ⓑ   75

Ⓒ   80

Ⓓ   90

54   Mrs. Williams is preparing lemonade for a birthday party. She wants each child to have exactly 2 cups of lemonade with no lemonade left over. She needs to use 4 lemons to make each cup of lemonade. How many lemons will she need to make enough lemonade for 12 children?

Ⓐ   6

Ⓑ   24

Ⓒ   48

Ⓓ   96

55   Which word best describes the shape of the sign below?

Ⓐ   Scalene

Ⓑ   Equilateral

Ⓒ   Isosceles

Ⓓ   Right

56   Carmen tossed a coin 10 times. The coin landed on heads 6 times and tails 4 times. She wants to complete the tally chart below to show the results.

Heads	Tails

Which of these should Carmen place in the "Heads" column?

Ⓐ | | | |

Ⓑ   卌

Ⓒ   卌 |

Ⓓ   卌 | |

57   Lisa filled the box below with 1-centimeter cubes. How many 1-centimeter cubes would it take to fill the box?

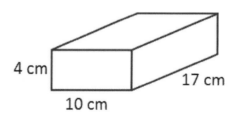

Ⓐ   160

Ⓑ   556

Ⓒ   680

Ⓓ   1,020

58   The stem-and-leaf plot shows the noon temperature each day over a 3-week period for Greenville.

Temperature at Noon (°C)

Stem	Leaf
1	9 9
2	2 4 5 6 7 7 7 7 8 8 9 9 9
3	0 0 1 1 1 2

What was the difference, in °C, between the highest and lowest temperature? Record your answer and fill in the bubbles on the grid. Be sure to use the correct place value.

59   Which calculation is represented on the grid below?

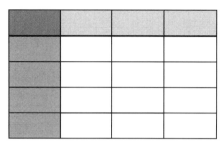

   Ⓐ $0.25 \div 0.2$

   Ⓑ $0.25 \div 4$

   Ⓒ $0.2 \div 4$

   Ⓓ $0.2 \div 5$

60   Tim plotted four points on the coordinate grid below. Which point would be 5 units from the origin and on the *x*-axis?

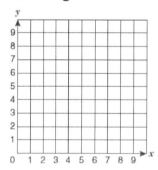

   Ⓐ   (0, 0)

   Ⓑ   (0, 5)

   Ⓒ   (5, 0)

   Ⓓ   (5, 5)

END OF TEST

STAAR Mathematics

Grade 5

Practice Test 2

Session 1

Directions

Read each question carefully. For a multiple-choice question, determine the best answer to the question from the four answer choices provided.

For a griddable question, determine the best answer. Write your answer at the top of the grid. Then shade the grid to show your answer.

You may use a ruler to help you answer questions. You may also use the information on the Reference Sheet at the back of this book. You may not use a calculator on this test.

---

1   Which number is the greatest?

Ⓐ   65.029

Ⓑ   65.061

Ⓒ   65.101

Ⓓ   65.125

2   Trevor's baby sister had a nap for $1\frac{3}{4}$ hours. How many minutes did she nap for? Record your answer and fill in the bubbles on the grid. Be sure to use the correct place value.

3   The decimal cards for 0.59 and 0.22 are shown below.

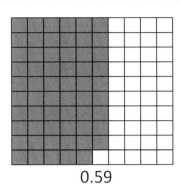   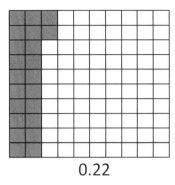

0.59   0.22

What is the difference of 0.59 and 0.22?

Ⓐ   0.39

Ⓑ   0.37

Ⓒ   0.81

Ⓓ   0.83

4   The table below shows a set of number pairs.

x	y
1	1
3	5
5	9

If the points were plotted on a coordinate grid, which of the following would be the coordinates of one of the points?

Ⓐ   (0, 0)

Ⓑ   (1, 3)

Ⓒ   (3, 5)

Ⓓ   (9, 5)

5   A fish tank can hold 20 liters of water. How many milliliters of water can the fish tank hold?

⒜   200 milliliters

Ⓑ   2,000 milliliters

Ⓒ   20,000 milliliters

Ⓓ   200,000 milliliters

6   A pattern of numbers is shown below.

8, 13, 18, 23, 28, 33, 38, …

Which of the following could be a number in the pattern?

⒜   80

Ⓑ   58

Ⓒ   42

Ⓓ   71

7   There are 200 students at Kerry's elementary school. Of those students, $\frac{2}{5}$ are fifth grade students. How many fifth grade students are there?

⒜   20

Ⓑ   40

Ⓒ   60

Ⓓ   80

8   Bryant was reading a book with 220 pages. He read 90 pages in the first week. He wants to finish the book in 5 days. Which expression can be used to calculate how many pages he needs to read each day to finish the book in 5 days?

Ⓐ $220 \div 5 - 90$

Ⓑ $220 - 90 \div 5$

Ⓒ $220 - (90 \div 5)$

Ⓓ $(220 - 90) \div 5$

9   Look at the fractions below.

$$1\frac{1}{3}, \ 2\frac{1}{2}, \ 3\frac{5}{6}$$

Which procedure can be used to find the sum of the fractions?

Ⓐ   Find the sum of the whole numbers, find the sum of the fractions, and then add the two sums

Ⓑ   Find the sum of the whole numbers, find the sum of the fractions, and then multiply the two sums

Ⓒ   Find the sum of the whole numbers, find the sum of the fractions, and then subtract the two sums

Ⓓ   Find the sum of the whole numbers, find the sum of the fractions, and then divide the two sums

10   The table below shows a set of number pairs.

x	y
1	1
3	5
5	9

Which equation shows the relationship between x and y?

Ⓐ $y = x + 2$

Ⓑ $y = x + 4$

Ⓒ $y = 2x - 1$

Ⓓ $y = 3x - 4$

11   Liam made 72 fluid ounces of lemonade for a party. How many cups of lemonade did Liam make?

Ⓐ   9 cups

Ⓑ   36 cups

Ⓒ   18 cups

Ⓓ   12 cups

12 The graph below shows data a science class collected on the diameter of hailstones that fell during a storm.

Hailstone Diameter (inches)

X								
X				X	X			
X	X		X	X	X	X	X	
0	$\frac{1}{8}$	$\frac{1}{4}$	$\frac{3}{8}$	$\frac{1}{2}$	$\frac{5}{8}$	$\frac{3}{4}$	$\frac{7}{8}$	1

How many hailstones had diameters of $\frac{1}{2}$ inch or more?

Ⓐ 2

Ⓑ 4

Ⓒ 6

Ⓓ 10

13 Joy made an apple pie. Joy and her 3 children ate $\frac{5}{8}$ of the apple pie. What fraction of the apple pie would be left over?

Ⓐ $\frac{9}{8}$

Ⓑ $\frac{3}{8}$

Ⓒ $\frac{5}{12}$

Ⓓ $\frac{5}{32}$

14   The graph below shows the line segment *PQ*. Point *P* is at (3, 9). Point *Q* is at (3, 1).

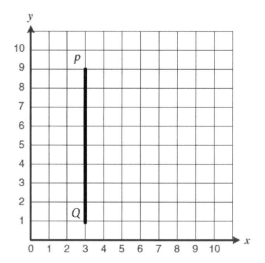

What is the length of the line segment *PQ*?

Ⓐ   3 units

Ⓑ   8 units

Ⓒ   9 units

Ⓓ   10 units

15   The factor tree for the number 36 is shown below.

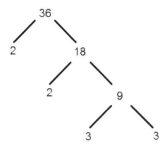

Which number is a prime factor of 36?

Ⓐ   3

Ⓑ   6

Ⓒ   9

Ⓓ   18

16   An orchard has a total of 1,176 orange trees. They are planted in rows of 12 orange trees each. How many rows of orange trees does the orchard have? Record your answer and fill in the bubbles on the grid. Be sure to use the correct place value.

			.		
0	0	0		0	0
1	1	1		1	1
2	2	2		2	2
3	3	3		3	3
4	4	4		4	4
5	5	5		5	5
6	6	6		6	6
7	7	7		7	7
8	8	8		8	8
9	9	9		9	9

17 Don spends $12.80 on four sandwiches. If each sandwich has the same cost, what is the cost of each sandwich?

Ⓐ $3.02

Ⓑ $3.20

Ⓒ $4.02

Ⓓ $4.20

18 Which number is a prime factor of the composite number 40?

Ⓐ   3

Ⓑ   5

Ⓒ   8

Ⓓ   10

19 Leanne added $\frac{1}{4}$ cup of milk and $\frac{3}{8}$ cup of water to a bowl. Which diagram is shaded to show how many cups of milk and water were in the bowl in all?

Ⓐ

Ⓑ

Ⓒ

Ⓓ

20   Which decimal is represented below?

$$(4 \times 100) + (8 \times 1) + (6 \times \frac{1}{100}) + (3 \times \frac{1}{1000})$$

Ⓐ   480.63

Ⓑ   480.063

Ⓒ   408.63

Ⓓ   408.063

21   A horse is 5 feet 2 inches high. How many inches high is the horse?

Ⓐ   60 inches

Ⓑ   62 inches

Ⓒ   80 inches

Ⓓ   82 inches

22   The graph below shows a line segment with 3 points marked.

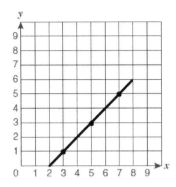

Which table shows the coordinates of these 3 points?

Ⓐ

x	1	2	3
y	3	5	7

Ⓑ

x	3	5	7
y	1	3	5

Ⓒ

x	1	3	5
y	1	2	3

Ⓓ

x	1	3	5
y	3	5	7

23   Brian made 16 paper cranes in 15 minutes. If he continues making cranes at this rate, how many cranes would he make in 2 hours?

Ⓐ   32

Ⓑ   64

Ⓒ   120

Ⓓ   128

24   The cost of renting a windsurfer is a basic fee of $15 plus an additional $5 for each hour that the windsurfer is rented. Which equation can be used to find c, the cost in dollars of the rental for h hours?

Ⓐ $c = 15h + 5$

Ⓑ $c = 5h + 15$

Ⓒ $c = 15(h + 5)$

Ⓓ $c = 5(h + 15)$

25 Amanda plotted the four points below on a coordinate grid.

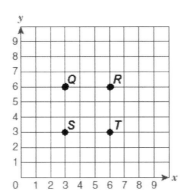

Amanda plots a fifth point that is an equal distance from two of the points. Which of these could be the coordinates of the fifth point?

(A)   (5, 8)

(B)   (3.5, 5)

(C)   (7, 7)

(D)   (9, 4.5)

26 Joy made 24 apple pies for a bake sale. Each serving was $\frac{1}{8}$ of a pie. How many servings did Joy make?

(A)   3

(B)   32

(C)   96

(D)   192

27   The model below is made up of 1-centimeter cubes. What is a correct way to find the volume of the cube, in cubic centimeters?

    Ⓐ   3 + 3 + 3

    Ⓑ   3 × 3 × 3

    Ⓒ   3 × 3

    Ⓓ   6(3 × 3)

28   What is the decimal 55.146 rounded to the nearest tenth?

    Ⓐ   55.1

    Ⓑ   55.2

    Ⓒ   55.14

    Ⓓ   55.15

29   Which ordered pair represents a point located on the line?

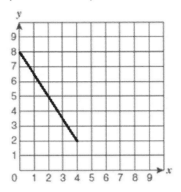

Ⓐ   (8, 0)

Ⓑ   (4, 2)

Ⓒ   (3, 3)

Ⓓ   (5, 2)

30   Hannah cut out a piece of fabric to use for an art project. The length of the fabric was 9.5 yards. The width of the fabric was 3.6 yards less than the length. What was the width of the fabric?

Ⓐ   5.9 yards

Ⓑ   6.9 yards

Ⓒ   12.1 yards

Ⓓ   13.1 yards

END OF SESSION 1

STAAR Mathematics

Grade 5

Practice Test 2

Session 2

Directions

Read each question carefully. For a multiple-choice question, determine the best answer to the question from the four answer choices provided.

For a griddable question, determine the best answer. Write your answer at the top of the grid. Then shade the grid to show your answer.

You may use a ruler to help you answer questions. You may also use the information on the Reference Sheet at the back of this book. You may not use a calculator on this test.

---

31   Which of these shapes has exactly one pair of perpendicular sides?

Ⓐ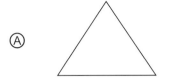

Ⓑ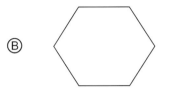

Ⓒ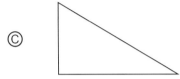

Ⓓ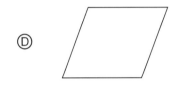

32   The table below shows the total number of lemons in different numbers of bags of lemons.

Number of Bags	Number of Lemons
2	16
3	24
5	40
8	64

What is the relationship between the number of bags of lemons and the total number of lemons?

Ⓐ   The number of lemons is 8 more than the number of bags.

Ⓑ   The number of lemons is 16 more than the number of bags.

Ⓒ   The number of lemons is 8 times the number of bags.

Ⓓ   The number of lemons is 16 times the number of bags.

33   Amy ordered 3 pizzas for $6.95 each. She also bought a soft drink for $1.95. Which equation can be used to find how much change, c, she should receive from $30?

Ⓐ $c = 30 - 3(6.95 + 1.95)$

Ⓑ $c = 30 - 3(6.95 - 1.95)$

Ⓒ $c = 30 - 6.95 - 1.95$

Ⓓ $c = 30 - (6.95 \times 3) - 1.95$

34   How is the numeral 55.12 written in words?

ⓐ   Fifty-five hundred and twelve

ⓑ   Fifty-five and twelve thousandths

ⓒ   Fifty-five and twelve hundredths

ⓓ   Fifty-five and twelve

35   Liam drew a triangle with no equal side lengths, as shown below.

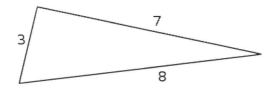

What type of triangle did Liam draw?

ⓐ   Scalene

ⓑ   Equilateral

ⓒ   Isosceles

ⓓ   Right

36   If $p = 5$, what is the value of $4(p + 7)$?

Ⓐ   27

Ⓑ   48

Ⓒ   52

Ⓓ   63

37   The table shows the side length of a rhombus and the perimeter of a rhombus.

Side Length, x (cm)	Perimeter, y (cm)
1	4
2	8
3	12
4	16

Which equation represents the relationship between side length and perimeter?

Ⓐ $y = x + 3$

Ⓑ $y = 4x$

Ⓒ $x = y + 4$

Ⓓ $x = 4y$

38   Frankie swims laps of her pool each morning. It takes her 1.25 minutes to swim one lap. How long would it would take Frankie to swim 15 laps?

    Ⓐ   12.5 minutes

    Ⓑ   13.75 minutes

    Ⓒ   15.25 minutes

    Ⓓ   18.75 minutes

39   Yuri makes $660 each week. He needs $380 to pay fixed expenses, $180 for spending, and plans to save the rest. How much can Yuri save each week?

    Ⓐ $80

    Ⓑ $100

    Ⓒ $160

    Ⓓ $280

40   It took James and his family $2\frac{1}{4}$ hours to drive from their house to the beach. How many minutes did the drive take?

    Ⓐ   175 minutes

    Ⓑ   75 minutes

    Ⓒ   120 minutes

    Ⓓ   135 minutes

41   The picture below represents a playground.

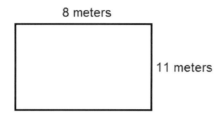

8 meters

11 meters

A fence is being built to go around the edge of the playground. The timber for the fence costs $14 per meter. If enough timber if bought to fit exactly around the edge of the playground, what will the total cost of the materials be, in dollars? Record your answer and fill in the bubbles on the grid. Be sure to use the correct place value.

			.		
⓪	⓪	⓪		⓪	⓪
①	①	①		①	①
②	②	②		②	②
③	③	③		③	③
④	④	④		④	④
⑤	⑤	⑤		⑤	⑤
⑥	⑥	⑥		⑥	⑥
⑦	⑦	⑦		⑦	⑦
⑧	⑧	⑧		⑧	⑧
⑨	⑨	⑨		⑨	⑨

42   Keegan's family 2 gallons of milk every week.

How many pints of milk does Keegan's family drink each week?

Ⓐ   4 pints

Ⓑ   8 pints

Ⓒ   16 pints

Ⓓ   32 pints

43   Evan's gross annual income is $37,000. Why is Evan's net income less than this?

Ⓐ   The net income is the gross income less taxes.

Ⓑ   The net income is the gross income less spending.

Ⓒ   The net income is the gross income less savings.

Ⓓ   The net income is the gross income less fixed expenses.

44   What is the value of the expression below?

$$42 + 24 \div 3 + 3$$

Ⓐ   22

Ⓑ   25

Ⓒ   46

Ⓓ   53

45   What is the volume of the model, in cubic units?

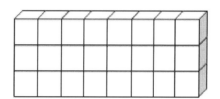

Record your answer and fill in the bubbles on the grid. Be sure to use the correct place value.

			.		
⓪	⓪	⓪		⓪	⓪
①	①	①		①	①
②	②	②		②	②
③	③	③		③	③
④	④	④		④	④
⑤	⑤	⑤		⑤	⑤
⑥	⑥	⑥		⑥	⑥
⑦	⑦	⑦		⑦	⑦
⑧	⑧	⑧		⑧	⑧
⑨	⑨	⑨		⑨	⑨

46 The mass of a car is 1.56 tons. What is the mass of the car in pounds?

Ⓐ 302 pounds

Ⓑ 312 pounds

Ⓒ 3,020 pounds

Ⓓ 3,120 pounds

47 A factory can fill 225 bottles of juice each hour. How many bottles of juice can be filled in each 12-hour shift?

Ⓐ 2,475

Ⓑ 2,600

Ⓒ 2,690

Ⓓ 2,700

48 A pattern has the rule $y = 2x + 4$. What is the value of y when $x = 5$?

Ⓐ 11

Ⓑ 14

Ⓒ 18

Ⓓ 30

49   Joshua bought a pair of sunglasses for $14.85 and a phone case for $2.55. How much change should he receive from $20, in dollars? Record your answer and fill in the bubbles on the grid. Be sure to use the correct place value.

			.		
⓪	⓪	⓪		⓪	⓪
①	①	①		①	①
②	②	②		②	②
③	③	③		③	③
④	④	④		④	④
⑤	⑤	⑤		⑤	⑤
⑥	⑥	⑥		⑥	⑥
⑦	⑦	⑦		⑦	⑦
⑧	⑧	⑧		⑧	⑧
⑨	⑨	⑨		⑨	⑨

50   Leo measures the length, width, and height of a block. He multiplies the length, width, and height. What is Leo finding?

Ⓐ   Surface area

Ⓑ   Mass

Ⓒ   Volume

Ⓓ   Perimeter

51 What is the decimal 38.647 rounded to the nearest hundredth?

Ⓐ 38.6

Ⓑ 38.7

Ⓒ 38.64

Ⓓ 38.65

52 The table shows the side length of a square and the area of a square.

Side Length, x (inches)	Area, y (square inches)
2	4
3	9
4	16
5	25

Which equation represents the relationship between side length and area?

Ⓐ $y = x + 2$

Ⓑ $y = 2x$

Ⓒ $y = x \times x$

Ⓓ $y = 4x$

53   The graph below shows the number of different types of trees in an orchard.

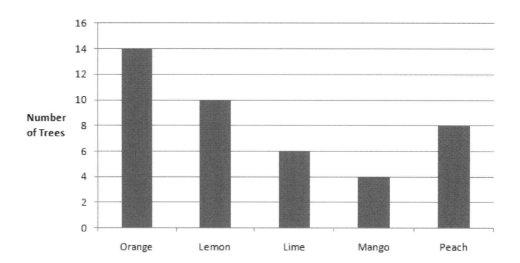

The owner wants to plant more trees so that there are 16 trees of each type. How many more trees does the owner need to plant?

Ⓐ   38

Ⓑ   28

Ⓒ   14

Ⓓ   10

54   Look at the triangles below.

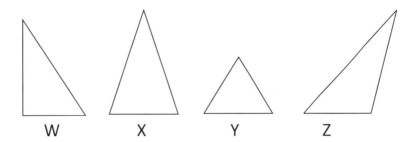

Connor classifies triangles X and Y as isosceles triangles because they have a pair of equal sides. What error has Connor made?

Ⓐ   He has not recognized that triangle Y has more than 2 equal sides.

Ⓑ   He has not considered the angle measures of triangle X.

Ⓒ   He has not recognized that triangle X only has 2 equal sides.

Ⓓ   He has not considered whether triangles X and Y have right angles.

55   Which situation would a stem-and-leaf plot best be used for?

Ⓐ   How the number of students at a school has changed over the years

Ⓑ   What fraction of people voted for each student in a school election

Ⓒ   How the age and height of students is related

Ⓓ   What score out of 100 thirty students got on a test

56   Annabelle has 56 1-centimeter cubes. What are the dimensions of a rectangular prism Annabelle could build with all the cubes?

Ⓐ   7 units long, 4 units high, 2 units wide

Ⓑ   6 units long, 5 units high, 5 units wide

Ⓒ   10 units long, 2 units high, 3 units wide

Ⓓ   8 units long, 2 units high, 4 units wide

57   The stem-and-leaf plot shows the amount in tips Cleo earned on each day that she worked in July.

Tips Earned ($)

Stem	Leaf
2	2 4 8 9
3	0 0 2 3 5 5 5 7 7 8 9
4	0 1 1 4 8
5	2 5

On how many days did Cleo earn more than $50 in tips?

Ⓐ   2

Ⓑ   7

Ⓒ   25

Ⓓ   55

58 Jezebel plots the point (3, 5) on a coordinate grid. Which of these describes where the point would be plotted?

(A)   3 units up from the origin and 5 units left of the *y*-axis

(B)   3 units up from the origin and 5 units right of the *y*-axis

(C)   3 units to the left of the origin and 5 units up from the *x*-axis

(D)   3 units to the right of the origin and 5 units up from the *x*-axis

59 Samantha worked for 40 hours at a rate of $15 per hour. She paid taxes of 20% on her gross income. What was Samantha's net income?

(A) $480

(B) $580

(C) $620

(D) $720

60 Which statement below is true?

(A)   0.06 < 0.006

(B)   1.22 < 1.42

(C)   5.669 < 5.667

(D)   7.535 < 7.505

END OF TEST

STAAR Mathematics

Grade 5

Practice Test 3

Session 1

Directions

Read each question carefully. For a multiple-choice question, determine the best answer to the question from the four answer choices provided.

For a griddable question, determine the best answer. Write your answer at the top of the grid. Then shade the grid to show your answer.

You may use a ruler to help you answer questions. You may also use the information on the Reference Sheet at the back of this book. You may not use a calculator on this test.

---

1   A pattern has the rule $y = 4x - 1$. What is the value of y when $x = 6$?

   (A)   9

   (B)   18

   (C)   20

   (D)   23

2   A cat weighs 9 pounds. How many ounces does the cat weigh?
Record your answer and fill in the bubbles on the grid. Be sure to use
the correct place value.

			.		
(0)	(0)	(0)		(0)	(0)
(1)	(1)	(1)		(1)	(1)
(2)	(2)	(2)		(2)	(2)
(3)	(3)	(3)		(3)	(3)
(4)	(4)	(4)		(4)	(4)
(5)	(5)	(5)		(5)	(5)
(6)	(6)	(6)		(6)	(6)
(7)	(7)	(7)		(7)	(7)
(8)	(8)	(8)		(8)	(8)
(9)	(9)	(9)		(9)	(9)

3   Jade does a household budget and finds she needs $565 each week to pay her expenses. Jade earns $485 each week after taxes. Which action could Jade take to balance the budget?

Ⓐ   Decrease her expenses by $80

Ⓑ   Decrease her earnings by $80

Ⓒ   Decrease her earnings by $80 and decrease her expenses by $80

Ⓓ   Increase her earnings by $80 and increase her expenses by $80

4   The top of a desk is 4 feet long and 3 feet wide. Raymond wants to find the area of the desk. What is the area of the top of the desk?

Ⓐ   12 square feet

Ⓑ   14 square feet

Ⓒ   16 square feet

Ⓓ   24 square feet

5 The cost of renting a trailer is a basic fee of $20 plus an additional $25 for each day that the trailer is rented. The cost, c, is represented by the equation below, where d is the number of days.

$$c = 25d + 20$$

How much would it cost to rent a trailer for 5 days?

Ⓐ $50

Ⓑ $145

Ⓒ $225

Ⓓ $625

6 Brett surveys students and asks them how long they studied for a test. He wants to make a chart to see if there is a relationship between the time studied and the test score. What type of chart would Brett be best to use?

Ⓐ   Dot plot

Ⓑ   Stem-and-leaf plot

Ⓒ   Scatterplot

Ⓓ   Bar graph

7   Which statement is true?

Ⓐ   48.06 < 47.65

Ⓑ   32.55 < 32.09

Ⓒ   27.09 < 27.16

Ⓓ   11.88 < 11.73

8   Gina states that the number 945 is a prime number. Which statement best explains how you can tell that Gina is incorrect?

Ⓐ   The number 945 can be evenly divided by 5.

Ⓑ   The number 945 is a three-digit number.

Ⓒ   The number 945 is an odd number.

Ⓓ   The number 945 is greater than 100.

9 Mike went on vacation to Ohio. When he left home, the odometer read 7,219.4 miles. When he returned home, the odometer read 8,192.6 miles. How many miles did Mike travel? Record your answer and fill in the bubbles on the grid. Be sure to use the correct place value.

			.		
⓪	⓪	⓪		⓪	⓪
①	①	①		①	①
②	②	②		②	②
③	③	③		③	③
④	④	④		④	④
⑤	⑤	⑤		⑤	⑤
⑥	⑥	⑥		⑥	⑥
⑦	⑦	⑦		⑦	⑦
⑧	⑧	⑧		⑧	⑧
⑨	⑨	⑨		⑨	⑨

10 There are 365 days in a year and 24 hours in a day. How many hours are there in a year?

Ⓐ 8,540

Ⓑ 8,560

Ⓒ 8,740

Ⓓ 8,760

11   A restaurant manager kept a record of the pieces of pie sold one week. He found that 0.2 of the pieces sold were cherry pie. If there were a total of 360 pieces of pie sold that week, how many pieces of cherry pie were sold?

Ⓐ   18

Ⓑ   36

Ⓒ   60

Ⓓ   72

12   A rectangular field has a length of 80 feet and a width of 40 feet. What is the perimeter of the field, in feet? Record your answer and fill in the bubbles on the grid. Be sure to use the correct place value.

			.		
⓪	⓪	⓪		⓪	⓪
①	①	①		①	①
②	②	②		②	②
③	③	③		③	③
④	④	④		④	④
⑤	⑤	⑤		⑤	⑤
⑥	⑥	⑥		⑥	⑥
⑦	⑦	⑦		⑦	⑦
⑧	⑧	⑧		⑧	⑧
⑨	⑨	⑨		⑨	⑨

13 Which of the following is a correct definition of a square?

Ⓐ A rectangle with two pairs of parallel sides

Ⓑ A rectangle with adjacent sides perpendicular

Ⓒ A rhombus with four equal sides

Ⓓ A rhombus with four right angles

14 What is the rule to find the value of a term in the sequence below?

Position, n	Value of Term
1	3
2	5
3	7
4	9

Ⓐ $4n - 4$

Ⓑ $3n$

Ⓒ $2n + 1$

Ⓓ $n + 2$

15   The table below shows the number of households in three different suburbs.

Suburb	Number of Households
Wellington	135,682
Ashton	179,441
Ellis	120,597

Which is the best estimate of the total number of households in the three suburbs, to the nearest ten thousand?

Ⓐ   400,000

Ⓑ   435,720

Ⓒ   436,000

Ⓓ   440,000

16   Ellen multiplies the number 3 by a fraction. The result is a number greater than 3. Which of these could be the fraction?

Ⓐ $1\frac{1}{4}$

Ⓑ $\frac{8}{9}$

Ⓒ $\frac{1}{6}$

Ⓓ $\frac{1}{2}$

17 How is the numeral 9.007 written in words?

Ⓐ Nine and seven tenths

Ⓑ Nine and seven thousandths

Ⓒ Nine and seven hundredths

Ⓓ Nine thousand and seven

18 The table below shows the shirt number of four players on a basketball team.

Player	Shirt Number
Don	12
Jamie	17
Curtis	22
Chan	9

Which player has a prime number for a shirt number?

Ⓐ Don

Ⓑ Jamie

Ⓒ Curtis

Ⓓ Chan

19   Ursula plotted the point (8, 6) on a coordinate grid. She then added a second point 2 units to the left of the first point and 3 units down. What are the coordinates of the second point?

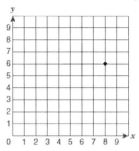

Ⓐ   (6, 3)

Ⓑ   (6, 9)

Ⓒ   (10, 3)

Ⓓ   (10, 9)

20   A diner sells 3 sizes of sodas. The table shows the number of sodas of each size sold in one day.

Size	Amount
Small	162
Medium	257
Large	188

Which of these is the closest estimate of how many more medium sodas the diner sold than small sodas?

Ⓐ   70

Ⓑ   80

Ⓒ   90

Ⓓ   100

21 The model below is made up of 1-centimeter cubes. What is the volume of the model, in cubic centimeters?

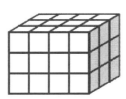

Record your answer and fill in the bubbles on the grid. Be sure to use the correct place value.

			.		
⓪	⓪	⓪		⓪	⓪
①	①	①		①	①
②	②	②		②	②
③	③	③		③	③
④	④	④		④	④
⑤	⑤	⑤		⑤	⑤
⑥	⑥	⑥		⑥	⑥
⑦	⑦	⑦		⑦	⑦
⑧	⑧	⑧		⑧	⑧
⑨	⑨	⑨		⑨	⑨

22   Which two shapes below should be placed in the overlapping section of the Venn diagram?

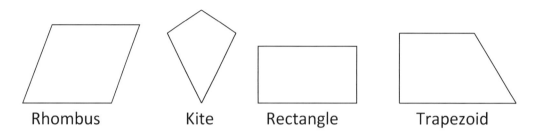

Rhombus   Kite   Rectangle   Trapezoid

At least 1 pair of parallel sides   At least 1 pair of congruent sides

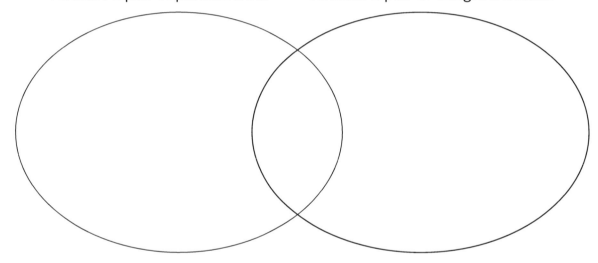

    Ⓐ   Rhombus and Trapezoid

    Ⓑ   Rhombus and Rectangle

    Ⓒ   Rectangle and Kite

    Ⓓ   Trapezoid and Kite

23   An Italian restaurant sells four types of meals. The owner made this graph to show how many meals of each type were sold one night.

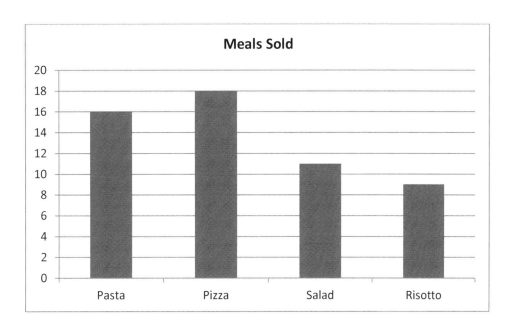

According to the graph, which statement is true?

Ⓐ   The store sold more pizza meals than salad and risotto meals combined.

Ⓑ   The store sold twice as many pizza meals as risotto meals.

Ⓒ   The store sold more pasta meals than any other type of meal.

Ⓓ   The store sold half as many salad meals as pasta meals.

24 At the start of the week, a plant had a height of $\frac{5}{8}$ inches. The plant grew $\frac{1}{4}$ of an inch during the week. Which diagram is shaded to show the height of the plant at the end of the week?

Ⓐ

Ⓑ

Ⓒ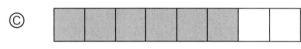

Ⓓ

25 How many millimeters are equivalent to 600 centimeters?

Ⓐ   0.6 mm

Ⓑ   6 mm

Ⓒ   60 mm

Ⓓ   6,000 mm

26   The grid below represents a garden.

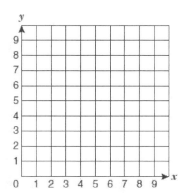

A lemon tree is located at the point (5, 4). An orange tree is located 4 units to the left of the lemon tree. Which ordered pair represents the location of the orange tree?

Ⓐ   (9, 4)

Ⓑ   (1, 4)

Ⓒ   (5, 9)

Ⓓ   (5, 0)

27   The table below shows the prices of items at a cake stall.

Item	Price
Small cake	$1.85
Muffin	$2.25
Cookie	$0.95

Frankie bought a small cake and a cookie. Bronwyn bought a muffin. How much more, in dollars, did Frankie spend than Bronwyn? Record your answer and fill in the bubbles on the grid. Be sure to use the correct place value.

			.		
⓪①②③④⑤⑥⑦⑧⑨	⓪①②③④⑤⑥⑦⑧⑨	⓪①②③④⑤⑥⑦⑧⑨		⓪①②③④⑤⑥⑦⑧⑨	⓪①②③④⑤⑥⑦⑧⑨

28 Harris saved $156 in 26 weeks. He saved the same amount of money each week. How much money did Harris save each week?

Ⓐ $4

Ⓑ $6

Ⓒ $8

Ⓓ $12

29 The table shows the side length of an equilateral triangle and the perimeter of an equilateral triangle.

Side Length, *l* (inches)	Perimeter, *P* (inches)
2	6
3	9
4	12
5	15

Which equation represents the relationship between side length and perimeter?

Ⓐ $P = l + 4$

Ⓑ $P = 3l$

Ⓒ $l = P + 4$

Ⓓ $l = 3P$

30   What is the value of 3.99 ÷ 30?

Ⓐ   1.33

Ⓑ   1.133

Ⓒ   0.133

Ⓓ   0.0133

END OF SESSION 1

STAAR Mathematics

Grade 5

Practice Test 3

Session 2

Directions

Read each question carefully. For a multiple-choice question, determine the best answer to the question from the four answer choices provided.

For a griddable question, determine the best answer. Write your answer at the top of the grid. Then shade the grid to show your answer.

You may use a ruler to help you answer questions. You may also use the information on the Reference Sheet at the back of this book. You may not use a calculator on this test.

31   The table below shows a set of number pairs.

x	y
2	−2
3	0
4	2

If the points were plotted on a coordinate grid, which of the following would be the coordinates of one of the points?

Ⓐ   (0, 2)

Ⓑ   (2, 2)

Ⓒ   (4, 2)

Ⓓ   (3, 4)

32   Dominic pays his local council tax on a block of land he owns each year. What type of tax is this?

Ⓐ   Income tax

Ⓑ   Payroll tax

Ⓒ   Property tax

Ⓓ   Sales tax

33 The table below shows the total cost of hiring DVDs for different numbers of DVDs.

Number of DVDs	Total Cost
2	$6
5	$15
6	$18
8	$24

What is the relationship between the number of DVDs hired and the total cost in dollars?

Ⓐ   The total cost is 3 times the number of DVDs.

Ⓑ   The total cost is 6 times the number of DVDs.

Ⓒ   The total cost is 4 more than the number of DVDs.

Ⓓ   The total cost is 10 more than the number of DVDs.

34   Donna has $8.45 in her purse. She spends $3.75. How much money, in dollars, does Donna have left? Record your answer and fill in the bubbles on the grid. Be sure to use the correct place value.

			.		
⓪	⓪	⓪		⓪	⓪
①	①	①		①	①
②	②	②		②	②
③	③	③		③	③
④	④	④		④	④
⑤	⑤	⑤		⑤	⑤
⑥	⑥	⑥		⑥	⑥
⑦	⑦	⑦		⑦	⑦
⑧	⑧	⑧		⑧	⑧
⑨	⑨	⑨		⑨	⑨

35   Mr. Singh bought 2 adult zoo tickets for a total of $22, as well as 4 children's tickets. He spent $54 in total. How much was each children's ticket?

Ⓐ $8

Ⓑ $2.50

Ⓒ $9

Ⓓ $13.50

36   Joanne had three singing lessons one week. Two lessons went for 45 minutes, and one lesson went for 60 minutes. Which number sentence could be used to find how many minutes Joanne had singing lessons for?

Ⓐ   (2 x 45) x 60

Ⓑ   (2 + 45) x 60

Ⓒ   (2 x 45) + 60

Ⓓ   (2 + 45) + 60

37   Jason used cubes to make the model shown below. What is the volume of the model?

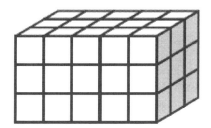

Ⓐ   15 cubic units

Ⓑ   45 cubic units

Ⓒ   50 cubic units

Ⓓ   75 cubic units

38   The grid below represents the calculation of 0.4 × 0.2.

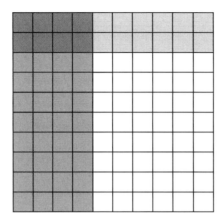

What is the value of 0.4 × 0.2? Record your answer and fill in the bubbles on the grid. Be sure to use the correct place value.

39 Emily cooked a roast on high for $1\frac{1}{4}$ hours. She then cooked it for another $\frac{1}{2}$ hour on low. How many minutes did she cook the roast for in all?

Ⓐ   75 minutes

Ⓑ   90 minutes

Ⓒ   105 minutes

Ⓓ   120 minutes

40 Which operation in the expression should be carried out first?

$$42 + 24 \div (3 - 1) \times 5$$

Ⓐ $42 + 24$

Ⓑ $24 \div 3$

Ⓒ $3 - 1$

Ⓓ 1×5

41 A bulldog weighs 768 ounces. How many pounds does the bulldog weigh?

Ⓐ   192 pounds

Ⓑ   48 pounds

Ⓒ   64 pounds

Ⓓ   96 pounds

42 Which two shapes have the same number of sides?

Ⓐ   Triangle and rectangle

Ⓑ   Rectangle and square

Ⓒ   Hexagon and pentagon

Ⓓ   Pentagon and triangle

43   Jasper made a flag for his football team. He painted $\frac{1}{2}$ of the flag blue. He divided the blue section into three equal parts and painted stars on one of the parts. What fraction of the total flag is the blue section with stars?

Ⓐ $\frac{1}{3}$

Ⓑ $\frac{1}{5}$

Ⓒ $\frac{1}{6}$

Ⓓ $\frac{1}{9}$

44   Maxwell bought a packet of 36 baseball cards. He gave 3 baseball cards to each of 4 friends. Which number sentence can be used to find c, the number of baseball cards Maxwell has left?

Ⓐ $36 + (3 + 4) = c$

Ⓑ $36 + (3 \times 4) = c$

Ⓒ $36 - (3 + 4) = c$

Ⓓ $36 - (3 \times 4) = c$

45   A piece of note paper has side lengths of 12.5 centimeters. What is the area of the piece of note paper?

Ⓐ   144.25 square centimeters

Ⓑ   144.5 square centimeters

Ⓒ   156.25 square centimeters

Ⓓ   156.5 square centimeters

46   A block is in the shape of a cube. If the side length is represented by *s*, which of these could be used to find the volume of the cube?

Ⓐ   3*s*

Ⓑ   6(*s* × *s*)

Ⓒ   6*s*

Ⓓ   *s* × *s* × *s*

47 Denise made the line plot below to show how long she read for each weekday for 4 weeks.

Daily Reading Time (hours)

How long did Denise read for in total over the 4 weeks?

Ⓐ   8 hours

Ⓑ   9 hours

Ⓒ   10 hours

Ⓓ   11 hours

48   Cody drew a quadrilateral on a coordinate grid, as shown below.

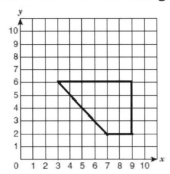

Which of these is **NOT** the coordinates of one of the vertices of the quadrilateral?

Ⓐ   (7, 2)

Ⓑ   (9, 2)

Ⓒ   (6, 9)

Ⓓ   (3, 6)

49   If the numbers below were each rounded to the nearest tenth, which number would be rounded down?

Ⓐ   17.386

Ⓑ   35.682

Ⓒ   23.758

Ⓓ   76.935

50   The diagram below shows the length of a piece of ribbon.

$$\frac{12}{100} \text{ meter}$$

Victoria divides the ribbon into 4 equal pieces. What is the length of each piece of ribbon?

Ⓐ $\frac{2}{25}$ meter

Ⓑ $\frac{3}{25}$ meter

Ⓒ $\frac{12}{25}$ meter

Ⓓ $\frac{3}{100}$ meter

51   A pattern of numbers is shown below.

6, 11, 16, 21, 26, 31, 36, ...

If n is a number in the pattern, which rule can be used to find the next number in the pattern?

Ⓐ $n + 5$

Ⓑ $n - 5$

Ⓒ $n + 6$

Ⓓ $n - 6$

52   A class held a vote on where to go for a field trip. The results are shown below.

Location	Number of Votes
Museum	ⵀⵀ ⵀⵀ
Cinema	ⵀⵀ |
Zoo	ⵀⵀ ⵀⵀ ⵀⵀ ⵀⵀ
Town Hall	||||

Chen decides to make a circle graph to show the results. Which section would make up a quarter of the graph?

Ⓐ   Museum

Ⓑ   Cinema

Ⓒ   Zoo

Ⓓ   Town Hall

53   The graph below shows the high temperature in Dallas, Texas for five days.

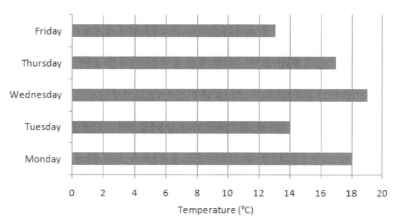

On which day was the high temperature 17°C?

Ⓐ   Tuesday

Ⓑ   Wednesday

Ⓒ   Thursday

Ⓓ   Friday

54   The graph below shows the line segment *ST*. Point *S* is at (2, 5). Point *T* is at (9, 5).

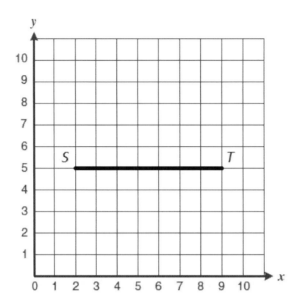

Which of these shows how to find the length of the line segment?

Ⓐ   5 + 5

Ⓑ   9 – 5

Ⓒ   9 – 2

Ⓓ   2 + 9

55 The table below shows the relationship between the original price and the sale price of a book.

Original price, *P*	Sale price, *S*
$10	$7.50
$12	$9
$14	$10.50
$16	$12

What is the rule to find the sale price of a book, in dollars?

Ⓐ $S = 0.25P$

Ⓑ $S = 0.75P$

Ⓒ $S = P - 2.5$

Ⓓ $S = P - 7.5$

56 Which shape represented below does **NOT** always have at least one pair of congruent sides?

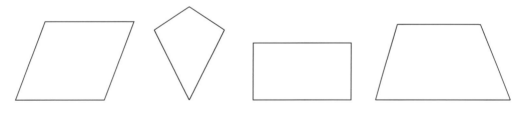

Ⓐ   Rhombus

Ⓑ   Kite

Ⓒ   Rectangle

Ⓓ   Trapezoid

57 Which decimal is represented below?

$$(6 \times 10) + (3 \times 1) + (9 \times \frac{1}{10}) + (4 \times \frac{1}{1000})$$

Ⓐ   63.094

Ⓑ   63.904

Ⓒ   63.94

Ⓓ   63.9004

58 Jonah filled the box below with 1-inch cubes. How many 1-inch cubes would it take to fill the box?

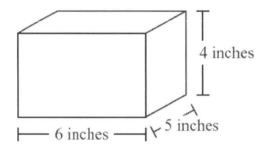

Ⓐ   15

Ⓑ   30

Ⓒ   60

Ⓓ   120

59 The dot plot below shows the number of athletics events entered by each student in a class.

Number of Athletics Events Entered

```
                        X
                        X         X
        X               X         X
        X       X       X         X
        X       X       X         X        X
        X       X       X         X        X
      _____
        1       2       3         4        5
```

What fraction of the students entered 5 events?

Ⓐ $\dfrac{1}{5}$

Ⓑ $\dfrac{1}{2}$

Ⓒ $\dfrac{1}{9}$

Ⓓ $\dfrac{1}{10}$

60   Which calculation is represented on the grid below?

(A) $0.1 \div 4$

(B) $0.25 \div 4$

(C) 0.1×4

(D) 0.25×4

END OF TEST

ANSWER KEY

About the Revised TEKS Standards

The STAAR Mathematics test assesses a specific set of skills. These are described in the Texas Essential Knowledge and Skills, or TEKS. Beginning with the 2014-2015 school year, student learning and assessment is based on the revised TEKS for mathematics. The questions in this book cover all the skills in the revised TEKS.

Reporting Categories and Skills

The TEKS standards are divided into four broad areas, known as Reporting Categories. On the state test, each category has a set amount of questions, with some categories having more questions than others. The Reporting Categories and the percentage of questions covering that category on the actual STAAR test are listed below.

Reporting Category	Percentage of Questions
Numerical Representations and Relationships	16%
Computations and Algebraic Relationships	48%
Geometry and Measurement	24%
Data Analysis and Personal Financial Literacy	12%

The answer key that follows includes the broad Reporting Category and the specific TEKS skill being assessed. These can be used to identify general areas of strength and weakness, as well as specific skills that the student is lacking. This information can then be used to target revision and instruction effectively.

STAAR Mathematics, Practice Test 1, Session 1

Question	Answer	Reporting Category	TEKS Skill
1	C	Data Analysis and Personal Financial Literacy	Solve one- and two-step problems using data from a frequency table, dot plot, bar graph, stem-and-leaf plot, or scatterplot.
2	33	Computations and Algebraic Relationships	Represent and solve multi-step problems involving the four operations with whole numbers using equations with a letter standing for the unknown quantity.
3	C	Computations and Algebraic Relationships	Represent division of a unit fraction by a whole number and the division of a whole number by a unit fraction such as $1/3 \div 7$ and $7 \div 1/3$ using objects and pictorial models, including area models.
4	C	Geometry and Measurement	Solve problems by calculating conversions within a measurement system, customary or metric.
5	B	Computations and Algebraic Relationships	Represent multiplication of decimals with products to the hundredths using objects and pictorial models, including area models.
6	C	Computations and Algebraic Relationships	Solve for products of decimals to the hundredths, including situations involving money, using strategies based on place-value understandings, properties of operations, and the relationship to the multiplication of whole numbers.
7	B	Geometry and Measurement	Describe the process for graphing ordered pairs of numbers in the first quadrant of the coordinate plane.
8	B	Numerical Representations and Relationships	Represent the value of the digit in decimals through the thousandths using expanded notation and numerals.
9	C	Geometry and Measurement	Graph in the first quadrant of the coordinate plane ordered pairs of numbers arising from mathematical and real-world problems, including those generated by number patterns or found in an input-output table.
10	A	Geometry and Measurement	Classify two-dimensional figures in a hierarchy of sets and subsets using graphic organizers based on their attributes and properties.

11	0.8	Computations and Algebraic Relationships	Add and subtract positive rational numbers fluently.
12	B	Geometry and Measurement	Solve problems by calculating conversions within a measurement system, customary or metric.
13	B	Data Analysis and Personal Financial Literacy	Represent discrete paired data on a scatterplot.
14	A	Computations and Algebraic Relationships	Represent and solve multi-step problems involving the four operations with whole numbers using equations with a letter standing for the unknown quantity.
15	D	Numerical Representations and Relationships	Describe the meaning of parentheses and brackets in a numeric expression.
16	A	Numerical Representations and Relationships	Identify prime and composite numbers.
17	C	Computations and Algebraic Relationships	Represent and solve addition and subtraction of fractions with unequal denominators referring to the same whole using objects and pictorial models and properties of operations.
18	A	Geometry and Measurement	Classify two-dimensional figures in a hierarchy of sets and subsets using graphic organizers based on their attributes and properties.
19	C	Computations and Algebraic Relationships	Divide whole numbers by unit fractions and unit fractions by whole numbers.
20	D	Numerical Representations and Relationships	Identify prime and composite numbers.
21	C	Computations and Algebraic Relationships	Recognize the difference between additive and multiplicative numerical patterns given in a table or graph.
22	C	Computations and Algebraic Relationships	Represent and solve multiplication of a whole number and a fraction that refers to the same whole using objects and pictorial models, including area models.
23	C	Geometry and Measurement	Recognize a cube with side length of one unit as a unit cube having one cubic unit of volume and the volume of a three-dimensional figure as the number of unit cubes (n cubic units) needed to fill it with no gaps or overlaps if possible.

24	C	Geometry and Measurement	Solve problems by calculating conversions within a measurement system, customary or metric.
25	D	Numerical Representations and Relationships	Simplify numerical expressions that do not involve exponents, including up to two levels of grouping.
26	D	Geometry and Measurement	Represent and solve problems related to perimeter and/or area and related to volume.
27	14	Computations and Algebraic Relationships	Solve with proficiency for quotients of up to a four-digit dividend by a two-digit divisor using strategies and the standard algorithm.
28	A	Geometry and Measurement	Describe the key attributes of the coordinate plane, including perpendicular number lines (axes) where the intersection (origin) of the two lines coincides with zero on each number line and the given point (0, 0); the x-coordinate, the first number in an ordered pair, indicates movement parallel to the x-axis starting at the origin; and the y-coordinate, the second number, indicates movement parallel to the y-axis starting at the origin.
29	B	Geometry and Measurement	Classify two-dimensional figures in a hierarchy of sets and subsets using graphic organizers based on their attributes and properties.
30	A	Data Analysis and Personal Financial Literacy	Represent categorical data with bar graphs or frequency tables and numerical data, including data sets of measurements in fractions or decimals, with dot plots or stem-and-leaf plots.

STAAR Mathematics, Practice Test 1, Session 2

Question	Answer	Reporting Category	TEKS Skill
31	B	Computations and Algebraic Relationships	Solve for quotients of decimals to the hundredths, up to four-digit dividends and two-digit whole number divisors, using strategies and algorithms, including the standard algorithm.
32	D	Numerical Representations and Relationships	Round decimals to tenths or hundredths.
33	D	Computations and Algebraic Relationships	Represent and solve addition and subtraction of fractions with unequal denominators referring to the same whole using objects and pictorial models and properties of operations.
34	C	Data Analysis and Personal Financial Literacy	Define income tax, payroll tax, sales tax, and property tax.
35	B	Computations and Algebraic Relationships	Represent and solve multi-step problems involving the four operations with whole numbers using equations with a letter standing for the unknown quantity.
36	C	Numerical Representations and Relationships	Describe the meaning of parentheses and brackets in a numeric expression.
37	B	Computations and Algebraic Relationships	Represent multiplication of decimals with products to the hundredths using objects and pictorial models, including area models.
38	D	Geometry and Measurement	Graph in the first quadrant of the coordinate plane ordered pairs of numbers arising from mathematical and real-world problems, including those generated by number patterns or found in an input-output table.
39	A	Computations and Algebraic Relationships	Add and subtract positive rational numbers fluently.
40	D	Geometry and Measurement	Represent and solve problems related to perimeter and/or area and related to volume.
41	C	Computations and Algebraic Relationships	Estimate to determine solutions to mathematical and real-world problems involving addition, subtraction, multiplication, or division.

42	B	Computations and Algebraic Relationships	Solve for products of decimals to the hundredths, including situations involving money, using strategies based on place-value understandings, properties of operations, and the relationship to the multiplication of whole numbers.
43	B	Data Analysis and Personal Financial Literacy	Describe actions that might be taken to balance a budget when expenses exceed income.
44	B	Computations and Algebraic Relationships	Represent and solve addition and subtraction of fractions with unequal denominators referring to the same whole using objects and pictorial models and properties of operations.
45	B	Computations and Algebraic Relationships	Divide whole numbers by unit fractions and unit fractions by whole numbers.
46	B	Computations and Algebraic Relationships	Represent and solve multi-step problems involving the four operations with whole numbers using equations with a letter standing for the unknown quantity.
47	6.72	Geometry and Measurement	Solve problems by calculating conversions within a measurement system, customary or metric.
48	B	Geometry and Measurement	Determine the volume of a rectangular prism with whole number side lengths in problems related to the number of layers times the number of unit cubes in the area of the base.
49	C	Numerical Representations and Relationships	Simplify numerical expressions that do not involve exponents, including up to two levels of grouping.
50	B	Numerical Representations and Relationships	Compare and order two decimals to thousandths and represent comparisons using the symbols >, <, or =.
51	C	Data Analysis and Personal Financial Literacy	Solve one- and two-step problems using data from a frequency table, dot plot, bar graph, stem-and-leaf plot, or scatterplot.
52	D	Numerical Representations and Relationships	Round decimals to tenths or hundredths.
53	C	Computations and Algebraic Relationships	Represent and solve multiplication of a whole number and a fraction that refers to the same whole using objects and pictorial models, including area models.

54	D	Computations and Algebraic Relationships	Represent and solve multi-step problems involving the four operations with whole numbers using equations with a letter standing for the unknown quantity.
55	B	Geometry and Measurement	Classify two-dimensional figures in a hierarchy of sets and subsets using graphic organizers based on their attributes and properties.
56	C	Data Analysis and Personal Financial Literacy	Represent categorical data with bar graphs or frequency tables and numerical data, including data sets of measurements in fractions or decimals, with dot plots or stem-and-leaf plots.
57	C	Geometry and Measurement	Determine the volume of a rectangular prism with whole number side lengths in problems related to the number of layers times the number of unit cubes in the area of the base.
58	13	Data Analysis and Personal Financial Literacy	Solve one- and two-step problems using data from a frequency table, dot plot, bar graph, stem-and-leaf plot, or scatterplot.
59	C	Computations and Algebraic Relationships	Represent quotients of decimals to the hundredths, up to four-digit dividends and two-digit whole number divisors, using objects and pictorial models, including area models.
60	C	Geometry and Measurement	Describe the key attributes of the coordinate plane, including perpendicular number lines (axes) where the intersection (origin) of the two lines coincides with zero on each number line and the given point $(0, 0)$; the x-coordinate, the first number in an ordered pair, indicates movement parallel to the x-axis starting at the origin; and the y-coordinate, the second number, indicates movement parallel to the y-axis starting at the origin.

STAAR Mathematics, Practice Test 2, Session 1

Question	Answer	Reporting Category	TEKS Skill
1	D	Numerical Representations and Relationships	Compare and order two decimals to thousandths and represent comparisons using the symbols >, <, or =.
2	105	Computations and Algebraic Relationships	Represent and solve multiplication of a whole number and a fraction that refers to the same whole using objects and pictorial models, including area models.
3	B	Computations and Algebraic Relationships	Add and subtract positive rational numbers fluently.
4	C	Geometry and Measurement	Describe the process for graphing ordered pairs of numbers in the first quadrant of the coordinate plane.
5	C	Geometry and Measurement	Solve problems by calculating conversions within a measurement system, customary or metric.
6	B	Computations and Algebraic Relationships	Recognize the difference between additive and multiplicative numerical patterns given in a table or graph.
7	D	Computations and Algebraic Relationships	Represent and solve multiplication of a whole number and a fraction that refers to the same whole using objects and pictorial models, including area models.
8	D	Numerical Representations and Relationships	Describe the meaning of parentheses and brackets in a numeric expression.
9	A	Computations and Algebraic Relationships	Represent and solve addition and subtraction of fractions with unequal denominators referring to the same whole using objects and pictorial models and properties of operations.
10	C	Computations and Algebraic Relationships	Generate a numerical pattern when given a rule in the form $y = ax$ or $y = x + a$ and graph.
11	A	Geometry and Measurement	Solve problems by calculating conversions within a measurement system, customary or metric.
12	C	Data Analysis and Personal Financial Literacy	Represent categorical data with bar graphs or frequency tables and numerical data, including data sets of measurements in fractions or decimals, with dot plots or stem-and-leaf plots.

13	B	Computations and Algebraic Relationships	Represent and solve addition and subtraction of fractions with unequal denominators referring to the same whole using objects and pictorial models and properties of operations.
14	B	Geometry and Measurement	Describe the key attributes of the coordinate plane, including perpendicular number lines (axes) where the intersection (origin) of the two lines coincides with zero on each number line and the given point (0, 0); the x-coordinate, the first number in an ordered pair, indicates movement parallel to the x-axis starting at the origin; and the y-coordinate, the second number, indicates movement parallel to the y-axis starting at the origin.
15	A	Numerical Representations and Relationships	Identify prime and composite numbers.
16	98	Computations and Algebraic Relationships	Solve with proficiency for quotients of up to a four-digit dividend by a two-digit divisor using strategies and the standard algorithm.
17	B	Computations and Algebraic Relationships	Solve for quotients of decimals to the hundredths, up to four-digit dividends and two-digit whole number divisors, using strategies and algorithms, including the standard algorithm.
18	B	Numerical Representations and Relationships	Identify prime and composite numbers.
19	C	Computations and Algebraic Relationships	Represent and solve addition and subtraction of fractions with unequal denominators referring to the same whole using objects and pictorial models and properties of operations.
20	D	Numerical Representations and Relationships	Represent the value of the digit in decimals through the thousandths using expanded notation and numerals.
21	B	Geometry and Measurement	Solve problems by calculating conversions within a measurement system, customary or metric.
22	B	Geometry and Measurement	Graph in the first quadrant of the coordinate plane ordered pairs of numbers arising from mathematical and real-world problems, including those generated by number patterns or found in an input-output table.
23	D	Geometry and Measurement	Solve problems by calculating conversions within a measurement system, customary or metric.

24	B	Computations and Algebraic Relationships	Represent and solve multi-step problems involving the four operations with whole numbers using equations with a letter standing for the unknown quantity.
25	D	Geometry and Measurement	Describe the key attributes of the coordinate plane, including perpendicular number lines (axes) where the intersection (origin) of the two lines coincides with zero on each number line and the given point (0, 0); the x-coordinate, the first number in an ordered pair, indicates movement parallel to the x-axis starting at the origin; and the y-coordinate, the second number, indicates movement parallel to the y-axis starting at the origin.
26	D	Computations and Algebraic Relationships	Divide whole numbers by unit fractions and unit fractions by whole numbers.
27	B	Geometry and Measurement	Recognize a cube with side length of one unit as a unit cube having one cubic unit of volume and the volume of a three-dimensional figure as the number of unit cubes (n cubic units) needed to fill it with no gaps or overlaps if possible.
28	A	Numerical Representations and Relationships	Round decimals to tenths or hundredths.
29	B	Geometry and Measurement	Graph in the first quadrant of the coordinate plane ordered pairs of numbers arising from mathematical and real-world problems, including those generated by number patterns or found in an input-output table.
30	A	Computations and Algebraic Relationships	Add and subtract positive rational numbers fluently.

STAAR Mathematics, Practice Test 2, Session 2

Question	Answer	Reporting Category	TEKS Skill
31	C	Geometry and Measurement	Classify two-dimensional figures in a hierarchy of sets and subsets using graphic organizers based on their attributes and properties.
32	C	Computations and Algebraic Relationships	Recognize the difference between additive and multiplicative numerical patterns given in a table or graph.
33	D	Computations and Algebraic Relationships	Represent and solve multi-step problems involving the four operations with whole numbers using equations with a letter standing for the unknown quantity.
34	C	Numerical Representations and Relationships	Represent the value of the digit in decimals through the thousandths using expanded notation and numerals.
35	A	Geometry and Measurement	Classify two-dimensional figures in a hierarchy of sets and subsets using graphic organizers based on their attributes and properties.
36	B	Numerical Representations and Relationships	Describe the meaning of parentheses and brackets in a numeric expression.
37	B	Computations and Algebraic Relationships	Recognize the difference between additive and multiplicative numerical patterns given in a table or graph.
38	D	Computations and Algebraic Relationships	Solve for products of decimals to the hundredths, including situations involving money, using strategies based on place-value understandings, properties of operations, and the relationship to the multiplication of whole numbers.
39	B	Data Analysis and Personal Financial Literacy	Balance a simple budget.
40	D	Computations and Algebraic Relationships	Represent and solve multiplication of a whole number and a fraction that refers to the same whole using objects and pictorial models, including area models.
41	532	Geometry and Measurement	Represent and solve problems related to perimeter and/or area and related to volume.
42	C	Geometry and Measurement	Solve problems by calculating conversions within a measurement system, customary or metric.

43	A	Data Analysis and Personal Financial Literacy	Explain the difference between gross income and net income.
44	D	Numerical Representations and Relationships	Simplify numerical expressions that do not involve exponents, including up to two levels of grouping.
45	24	Geometry and Measurement	Determine the volume of a rectangular prism with whole number side lengths in problems related to the number of layers times the number of unit cubes in the area of the base.
46	D	Computations and Algebraic Relationships	Solve for products of decimals to the hundredths, including situations involving money, using strategies based on place-value understandings, properties of operations, and the relationship to the multiplication of whole numbers.
47	D	Computations and Algebraic Relationships	Multiply with fluency a three-digit number by a two-digit number using the standard algorithm.
48	B	Computations and Algebraic Relationships	Generate a numerical pattern when given a rule in the form $y = ax$ or $y = x + a$ and graph.
49	2.60	Computations and Algebraic Relationships	Add and subtract positive rational numbers fluently.
50	C	Geometry and Measurement	Represent and solve problems related to perimeter and/or area and related to volume.
51	D	Numerical Representations and Relationships	Round decimals to tenths or hundredths.
52	C	Computations and Algebraic Relationships	Represent and solve multi-step problems involving the four operations with whole numbers using equations with a letter standing for the unknown quantity.
53	A	Data Analysis and Personal Financial Literacy	Solve one- and two-step problems using data from a frequency table, dot plot, bar graph, stem-and-leaf plot, or scatterplot.
54	A	Geometry and Measurement	Classify two-dimensional figures in a hierarchy of sets and subsets using graphic organizers based on their attributes and properties.
55	D	Data Analysis and Personal Financial Literacy	Represent categorical data with bar graphs or frequency tables and numerical data, including data sets of measurements in fractions or decimals, with dot plots or stem-and-leaf plots.

56	A	Geometry and Measurement	Determine the volume of a rectangular prism with whole number side lengths in problems related to the number of layers times the number of unit cubes in the area of the base.
57	A	Data Analysis and Personal Financial Literacy	Solve one- and two-step problems using data from a frequency table, dot plot, bar graph, stem-and-leaf plot, or scatterplot.
58	D	Geometry and Measurement	Describe the process for graphing ordered pairs of numbers in the first quadrant of the coordinate plane.
59	A	Data Analysis and Personal Financial Literacy	Explain the difference between gross income and net income.
60	B	Numerical Representations and Relationships	Compare and order two decimals to thousandths and represent comparisons using the symbols >, <, or =.

STAAR Mathematics, Practice Test 3, Session 1

Question	Answer	Reporting Category	TEKS Skill
1	D	Computations and Algebraic Relationships	Generate a numerical pattern when given a rule in the form $y = ax$ or $y = x + a$ and graph.
2	144	Geometry and Measurement	Solve problems by calculating conversions within a measurement system, customary or metric.
3	A	Data Analysis and Personal Financial Literacy	Balance a simple budget.
4	A	Geometry and Measurement	Represent and solve problems related to perimeter and/or area and related to volume.
5	B	Computations and Algebraic Relationships	Represent and solve multi-step problems involving the four operations with whole numbers using equations with a letter standing for the unknown quantity.
6	C	Data Analysis and Personal Financial Literacy	Represent discrete paired data on a scatterplot.
7	C	Numerical Representations and Relationships	Compare and order two decimals to thousandths and represent comparisons using the symbols >, <, or =.
8	A	Numerical Representations and Relationships	Identify prime and composite numbers.
9	973.2	Computations and Algebraic Relationships	Add and subtract positive rational numbers fluently.
10	D	Computations and Algebraic Relationships	Multiply with fluency a three-digit number by a two-digit number using the standard algorithm.
11	D	Computations and Algebraic Relationships	Solve for products of decimals to the hundredths, including situations involving money, using strategies based on place-value understandings, properties of operations, and the relationship to the multiplication of whole numbers.
12	240	Geometry and Measurement	Represent and solve problems related to perimeter and/or area and related to volume.
13	D	Geometry and Measurement	Classify two-dimensional figures in a hierarchy of sets and subsets using graphic organizers based on their attributes and properties.
14	C	Computations and Algebraic Relationships	Generate a numerical pattern when given a rule in the form $y = ax$ or $y = x + a$ and graph.

15	D	Computations and Algebraic Relationships	Estimate to determine solutions to mathematical and real-world problems involving addition, subtraction, multiplication, or division.
16	A	Computations and Algebraic Relationships	Represent and solve multiplication of a whole number and a fraction that refers to the same whole using objects and pictorial models, including area models.
17	B	Numerical Representations and Relationships	Represent the value of the digit in decimals through the thousandths using expanded notation and numerals.
18	B	Numerical Representations and Relationships	Identify prime and composite numbers.
19	A	Geometry and Measurement	Describe the key attributes of the coordinate plane, including perpendicular number lines (axes) where the intersection (origin) of the two lines coincides with zero on each number line and the given point (0, 0); the x-coordinate, the first number in an ordered pair, indicates movement parallel to the x-axis starting at the origin; and the y-coordinate, the second number, indicates movement parallel to the y-axis starting at the origin.
20	D	Computations and Algebraic Relationships	Estimate to determine solutions to mathematical and real-world problems involving addition, subtraction, multiplication, or division.
21	36	Geometry and Measurement	Recognize a cube with side length of one unit as a unit cube having one cubic unit of volume and the volume of a three-dimensional figure as the number of unit cubes (n cubic units) needed to fill it with no gaps or overlaps if possible.
22	B	Geometry and Measurement	Classify two-dimensional figures in a hierarchy of sets and subsets using graphic organizers based on their attributes and properties.
23	B	Data Analysis and Personal Financial Literacy	Solve one- and two-step problems using data from a frequency table, dot plot, bar graph, stem-and-leaf plot, or scatterplot.
24	D	Computations and Algebraic Relationships	Represent and solve addition and subtraction of fractions with unequal denominators referring to the same whole using objects and pictorial models and properties of operations.
25	D	Geometry and Measurement	Solve problems by calculating conversions within a measurement system, customary or metric.

26	B	Geometry and Measurement	Graph in the first quadrant of the coordinate plane ordered pairs of numbers arising from mathematical and real-world problems, including those generated by number patterns or found in an input-output table.
27	0.55	Computations and Algebraic Relationships	Add and subtract positive rational numbers fluently.
28	B	Computations and Algebraic Relationships	Solve with proficiency for quotients of up to a four-digit dividend by a two-digit divisor using strategies and the standard algorithm.
29	B	Computations and Algebraic Relationships	Generate a numerical pattern when given a rule in the form $y = ax$ or $y = x + a$ and graph.
30	C	Computations and Algebraic Relationships	Solve for quotients of decimals to the hundredths, up to four-digit dividends and two-digit whole number divisors, using strategies and algorithms, including the standard algorithm.

STAAR Mathematics, Practice Test 3, Session 2

Question	Answer	Reporting Category	TEKS Skill
31	C	Geometry and Measurement	Describe the process for graphing ordered pairs of numbers in the first quadrant of the coordinate plane.
32	C	Data Analysis and Personal Financial Literacy	Define income tax, payroll tax, sales tax, and property tax.
33	A	Computations and Algebraic Relationships	Recognize the difference between additive and multiplicative numerical patterns given in a table or graph.
34	4.70	Computations and Algebraic Relationships	Add and subtract positive rational numbers fluently.
35	A	Computations and Algebraic Relationships	Represent and solve multi-step problems involving the four operations with whole numbers using equations with a letter standing for the unknown quantity.
36	C	Numerical Representations and Relationships	Describe the meaning of parentheses and brackets in a numeric expression.
37	B	Geometry and Measurement	Determine the volume of a rectangular prism with whole number side lengths in problems related to the number of layers times the number of unit cubes in the area of the base.
38	0.08	Computations and Algebraic Relationships	Represent multiplication of decimals with products to the hundredths using objects and pictorial models, including area models.
39	C	Computations and Algebraic Relationships	Represent and solve addition and subtraction of fractions with unequal denominators referring to the same whole using objects and pictorial models and properties of operations.
40	C	Numerical Representations and Relationships	Simplify numerical expressions that do not involve exponents, including up to two levels of grouping.
41	B	Geometry and Measurement	Solve problems by calculating conversions within a measurement system, customary or metric.
42	B	Geometry and Measurement	Classify two-dimensional figures in a hierarchy of sets and subsets using graphic organizers based on their attributes and properties.

43	C	Computations and Algebraic Relationships	Divide whole numbers by unit fractions and unit fractions by whole numbers.
44	D	Computations and Algebraic Relationships	Represent and solve multi-step problems involving the four operations with whole numbers using equations with a letter standing for the unknown quantity.
45	C	Computations and Algebraic Relationships	Solve for products of decimals to the hundredths, including situations involving money, using strategies based on place-value understandings, properties of operations, and the relationship to the multiplication of whole numbers.
46	D	Geometry and Measurement	Recognize a cube with side length of one unit as a unit cube having one cubic unit of volume and the volume of a three-dimensional figure as the number of unit cubes (*n* cubic units) needed to fill it with no gaps or overlaps if possible.
47	C	Data Analysis and Personal Financial Literacy	Solve one- and two-step problems using data from a frequency table, dot plot, bar graph, stem-and-leaf plot, or scatterplot.
48	C	Geometry and Measurement	Graph in the first quadrant of the coordinate plane ordered pairs of numbers arising from mathematical and real-world problems, including those generated by number patterns or found in an input-output table.
49	D	Numerical Representations and Relationships	Round decimals to tenths or hundredths.
50	D	Computations and Algebraic Relationships	Represent and solve multiplication of a whole number and a fraction that refers to the same whole using objects and pictorial models, including area models.
51	A	Computations and Algebraic Relationships	Represent and solve multi-step problems involving the four operations with whole numbers using equations with a letter standing for the unknown quantity.
52	A	Data Analysis and Personal Financial Literacy	Solve one- and two-step problems using data from a frequency table, dot plot, bar graph, stem-and-leaf plot, or scatterplot.
53	C	Data Analysis and Personal Financial Literacy	Represent categorical data with bar graphs or frequency tables and numerical data, including data sets of measurements in fractions or decimals, with dot plots or stem-and-leaf plots.

54	C	Geometry and Measurement	Describe the key attributes of the coordinate plane, including perpendicular number lines (axes) where the intersection (origin) of the two lines coincides with zero on each number line and the given point (0, 0); the *x*-coordinate, the first number in an ordered pair, indicates movement parallel to the *x*-axis starting at the origin; and the *y*-coordinate, the second number, indicates movement parallel to the *y*-axis starting at the origin.
55	B	Computations and Algebraic Relationships	Recognize the difference between additive and multiplicative numerical patterns given in a table or graph.
56	D	Geometry and Measurement	Classify two-dimensional figures in a hierarchy of sets and subsets using graphic organizers based on their attributes and properties.
57	B	Numerical Representations and Relationships	Represent the value of the digit in decimals through the thousandths using expanded notation and numerals.
58	D	Geometry and Measurement	Determine the volume of a rectangular prism with whole number side lengths in problems related to the number of layers times the number of unit cubes in the area of the base.
59	D	Data Analysis and Personal Financial Literacy	Solve one- and two-step problems using data from a frequency table, dot plot, bar graph, stem-and-leaf plot, or scatterplot.
60	A	Computations and Algebraic Relationships	Represent quotients of decimals to the hundredths, up to four-digit dividends and two-digit whole number divisors, using objects and pictorial models, including area models.

Answer Sheet: Practice Test 1

Session 1

1	Ⓐ Ⓑ Ⓒ Ⓓ	11	Ⓐ Ⓑ Ⓒ Ⓓ	21	Ⓐ Ⓑ Ⓒ Ⓓ
2	_____	12	Ⓐ Ⓑ Ⓒ Ⓓ	22	Ⓐ Ⓑ Ⓒ Ⓓ
3	Ⓐ Ⓑ Ⓒ Ⓓ	13	Ⓐ Ⓑ Ⓒ Ⓓ	23	Ⓐ Ⓑ Ⓒ Ⓓ
4	Ⓐ Ⓑ Ⓒ Ⓓ	14	Ⓐ Ⓑ Ⓒ Ⓓ	24	Ⓐ Ⓑ Ⓒ Ⓓ
5	Ⓐ Ⓑ Ⓒ Ⓓ	15	Ⓐ Ⓑ Ⓒ Ⓓ	25	Ⓐ Ⓑ Ⓒ Ⓓ
6	Ⓐ Ⓑ Ⓒ Ⓓ	16	Ⓐ Ⓑ Ⓒ Ⓓ	26	Ⓐ Ⓑ Ⓒ Ⓓ
7	Ⓐ Ⓑ Ⓒ Ⓓ	17	Ⓐ Ⓑ Ⓒ Ⓓ	27	_____
8	_____	18	Ⓐ Ⓑ Ⓒ Ⓓ	28	Ⓐ Ⓑ Ⓒ Ⓓ
9	Ⓐ Ⓑ Ⓒ Ⓓ	19	Ⓐ Ⓑ Ⓒ Ⓓ	29	Ⓐ Ⓑ Ⓒ Ⓓ
10	Ⓐ Ⓑ Ⓒ Ⓓ	20	Ⓐ Ⓑ Ⓒ Ⓓ	30	Ⓐ Ⓑ Ⓒ Ⓓ

Session 2

31	Ⓐ Ⓑ Ⓒ Ⓓ	41	Ⓐ Ⓑ Ⓒ Ⓓ	51	Ⓐ Ⓑ Ⓒ Ⓓ
32	Ⓐ Ⓑ Ⓒ Ⓓ	42	Ⓐ Ⓑ Ⓒ Ⓓ	52	Ⓐ Ⓑ Ⓒ Ⓓ
33	Ⓐ Ⓑ Ⓒ Ⓓ	43	Ⓐ Ⓑ Ⓒ Ⓓ	53	Ⓐ Ⓑ Ⓒ Ⓓ
34	Ⓐ Ⓑ Ⓒ Ⓓ	44	Ⓐ Ⓑ Ⓒ Ⓓ	54	Ⓐ Ⓑ Ⓒ Ⓓ
35	Ⓐ Ⓑ Ⓒ Ⓓ	45	Ⓐ Ⓑ Ⓒ Ⓓ	55	Ⓐ Ⓑ Ⓒ Ⓓ
36	Ⓐ Ⓑ Ⓒ Ⓓ	46	Ⓐ Ⓑ Ⓒ Ⓓ	56	Ⓐ Ⓑ Ⓒ Ⓓ
37	Ⓐ Ⓑ Ⓒ Ⓓ	47	_____	57	Ⓐ Ⓑ Ⓒ Ⓓ
38	Ⓐ Ⓑ Ⓒ Ⓓ	48	Ⓐ Ⓑ Ⓒ Ⓓ	58	_____
39	Ⓐ Ⓑ Ⓒ Ⓓ	49	Ⓐ Ⓑ Ⓒ Ⓓ	59	Ⓐ Ⓑ Ⓒ Ⓓ
40	Ⓐ Ⓑ Ⓒ Ⓓ	50	Ⓐ Ⓑ Ⓒ Ⓓ	60	Ⓐ Ⓑ Ⓒ Ⓓ

Answer Sheet: Practice Test 2

Session 1

1	Ⓐ Ⓑ Ⓒ Ⓓ	11	Ⓐ Ⓑ Ⓒ Ⓓ	21	Ⓐ Ⓑ Ⓒ Ⓓ
2	_____	12	Ⓐ Ⓑ Ⓒ Ⓓ	22	Ⓐ Ⓑ Ⓒ Ⓓ
3	Ⓐ Ⓑ Ⓒ Ⓓ	13	Ⓐ Ⓑ Ⓒ Ⓓ	23	Ⓐ Ⓑ Ⓒ Ⓓ
4	Ⓐ Ⓑ Ⓒ Ⓓ	14	Ⓐ Ⓑ Ⓒ Ⓓ	24	Ⓐ Ⓑ Ⓒ Ⓓ
5	Ⓐ Ⓑ Ⓒ Ⓓ	15	Ⓐ Ⓑ Ⓒ Ⓓ	25	Ⓐ Ⓑ Ⓒ Ⓓ
6	Ⓐ Ⓑ Ⓒ Ⓓ	16	_____	26	Ⓐ Ⓑ Ⓒ Ⓓ
7	Ⓐ Ⓑ Ⓒ Ⓓ	17	Ⓐ Ⓑ Ⓒ Ⓓ	27	Ⓐ Ⓑ Ⓒ Ⓓ
8	Ⓐ Ⓑ Ⓒ Ⓓ	18	Ⓐ Ⓑ Ⓒ Ⓓ	28	Ⓐ Ⓑ Ⓒ Ⓓ
9	Ⓐ Ⓑ Ⓒ Ⓓ	19	Ⓐ Ⓑ Ⓒ Ⓓ	29	Ⓐ Ⓑ Ⓒ Ⓓ
10	Ⓐ Ⓑ Ⓒ Ⓓ	20	Ⓐ Ⓑ Ⓒ Ⓓ	30	Ⓐ Ⓑ Ⓒ Ⓓ

Session 2

31	Ⓐ Ⓑ Ⓒ Ⓓ	41	_____	51	Ⓐ Ⓑ Ⓒ Ⓓ
32	Ⓐ Ⓑ Ⓒ Ⓓ	42	Ⓐ Ⓑ Ⓒ Ⓓ	52	Ⓐ Ⓑ Ⓒ Ⓓ
33	Ⓐ Ⓑ Ⓒ Ⓓ	43	Ⓐ Ⓑ Ⓒ Ⓓ	53	Ⓐ Ⓑ Ⓒ Ⓓ
34	Ⓐ Ⓑ Ⓒ Ⓓ	44	Ⓐ Ⓑ Ⓒ Ⓓ	54	Ⓐ Ⓑ Ⓒ Ⓓ
35	Ⓐ Ⓑ Ⓒ Ⓓ	45	_____	55	Ⓐ Ⓑ Ⓒ Ⓓ
36	Ⓐ Ⓑ Ⓒ Ⓓ	46	Ⓐ Ⓑ Ⓒ Ⓓ	56	Ⓐ Ⓑ Ⓒ Ⓓ
37	Ⓐ Ⓑ Ⓒ Ⓓ	47	Ⓐ Ⓑ Ⓒ Ⓓ	57	Ⓐ Ⓑ Ⓒ Ⓓ
38	Ⓐ Ⓑ Ⓒ Ⓓ	48	Ⓐ Ⓑ Ⓒ Ⓓ	58	Ⓐ Ⓑ Ⓒ Ⓓ
39	Ⓐ Ⓑ Ⓒ Ⓓ	49	_____	59	Ⓐ Ⓑ Ⓒ Ⓓ
40	Ⓐ Ⓑ Ⓒ Ⓓ	50	Ⓐ Ⓑ Ⓒ Ⓓ	60	Ⓐ Ⓑ Ⓒ Ⓓ

Answer Sheet: Practice Test 3

Session 1

1	Ⓐ Ⓑ Ⓒ Ⓓ	11	Ⓐ Ⓑ Ⓒ Ⓓ	21	_____
2	_____	12	_____	22	Ⓐ Ⓑ Ⓒ Ⓓ
3	Ⓐ Ⓑ Ⓒ Ⓓ	13	Ⓐ Ⓑ Ⓒ Ⓓ	23	Ⓐ Ⓑ Ⓒ Ⓓ
4	Ⓐ Ⓑ Ⓒ Ⓓ	14	Ⓐ Ⓑ Ⓒ Ⓓ	24	Ⓐ Ⓑ Ⓒ Ⓓ
5	Ⓐ Ⓑ Ⓒ Ⓓ	15	Ⓐ Ⓑ Ⓒ Ⓓ	25	Ⓐ Ⓑ Ⓒ Ⓓ
6	Ⓐ Ⓑ Ⓒ Ⓓ	16	Ⓐ Ⓑ Ⓒ Ⓓ	26	Ⓐ Ⓑ Ⓒ Ⓓ
7	Ⓐ Ⓑ Ⓒ Ⓓ	17	Ⓐ Ⓑ Ⓒ Ⓓ	27	_____
8	Ⓐ Ⓑ Ⓒ Ⓓ	18	Ⓐ Ⓑ Ⓒ Ⓓ	28	Ⓐ Ⓑ Ⓒ Ⓓ
9	_____	19	Ⓐ Ⓑ Ⓒ Ⓓ	29	Ⓐ Ⓑ Ⓒ Ⓓ
10	Ⓐ Ⓑ Ⓒ Ⓓ	20	Ⓐ Ⓑ Ⓒ Ⓓ	30	Ⓐ Ⓑ Ⓒ Ⓓ

Session 2

31	Ⓐ Ⓑ Ⓒ Ⓓ	41	Ⓐ Ⓑ Ⓒ Ⓓ	51	Ⓐ Ⓑ Ⓒ Ⓓ
32	Ⓐ Ⓑ Ⓒ Ⓓ	42	Ⓐ Ⓑ Ⓒ Ⓓ	52	Ⓐ Ⓑ Ⓒ Ⓓ
33	Ⓐ Ⓑ Ⓒ Ⓓ	43	Ⓐ Ⓑ Ⓒ Ⓓ	53	Ⓐ Ⓑ Ⓒ Ⓓ
34	_____	44	Ⓐ Ⓑ Ⓒ Ⓓ	54	Ⓐ Ⓑ Ⓒ Ⓓ
35	Ⓐ Ⓑ Ⓒ Ⓓ	45	Ⓐ Ⓑ Ⓒ Ⓓ	55	Ⓐ Ⓑ Ⓒ Ⓓ
36	Ⓐ Ⓑ Ⓒ Ⓓ	46	Ⓐ Ⓑ Ⓒ Ⓓ	56	Ⓐ Ⓑ Ⓒ Ⓓ
37	Ⓐ Ⓑ Ⓒ Ⓓ	47	Ⓐ Ⓑ Ⓒ Ⓓ	57	Ⓐ Ⓑ Ⓒ Ⓓ
38	_____	48	Ⓐ Ⓑ Ⓒ Ⓓ	58	Ⓐ Ⓑ Ⓒ Ⓓ
39	Ⓐ Ⓑ Ⓒ Ⓓ	49	Ⓐ Ⓑ Ⓒ Ⓓ	59	Ⓐ Ⓑ Ⓒ Ⓓ
40	Ⓐ Ⓑ Ⓒ Ⓓ	50	Ⓐ Ⓑ Ⓒ Ⓓ	60	Ⓐ Ⓑ Ⓒ Ⓓ

STAAR Grade 5 Mathematics Reference Sheet
You may use this information to help you answer questions.

PERIMETER

Square	$P = 4s$
Rectangle	$P = 2l + 2w$

AREA

Square			$A = s \times s$
Rectangle	$A = l \times w$	or	$A = bh$

VOLUME

Cube			$V = s \times s \times s$
Rectangular prism	$V = l \times w \times h$	or	$V = Bh$

LENGTH

Customary	Metric
1 mile (mi) = 1,760 yards (yd)	1 kilometer (km) = 1,000 meters (m)
1 yard (yd) = 3 feet (ft)	1 meter (m) = 100 centimeters (cm)
1 foot (ft) = 12 inches (in.)	1 centimeter (cm) = 10 millimeters (mm)

VOLUME AND CAPACITY

Customary	Metric
1 gallon (gal) = 4 quarts (qt)	1 liter (L) = 1,000 milliliters (mL)
1 quart (qt) = 2 pints (pt)	
1 pint (pt) = 2 cups (c)	
1 cup (c) = 8 fluid ounces (fl oz)	

WEIGHT AND MASS

Customary	Metric
1 ton (T) = 2,000 pounds (lb)	1 kilogram (kg) = 1,000 grams (g)
1 pound (lb) = 16 ounces (oz)	1 gram (g) = 1,000 milligrams (mg)

Get to Know Our Product Range

Mathematics

Practice Test Books
Practice sets and practice tests will prepare students for the state tests.

Quiz Books
Focused individual quizzes cover every math skill one by one.

 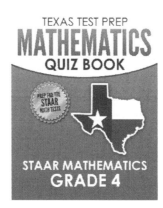 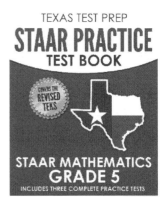

Reading

Practice Test Books
Practice sets and practice tests will prepare students for the state tests.

Reading Skills Workbooks
Short passages and question sets will develop and improve reading comprehension skills and are perfect for ongoing test prep.

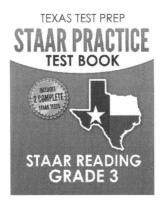 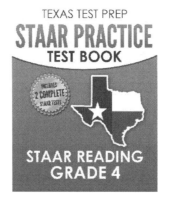 

Writing

Writing Skills Workbooks
Students write narratives, essays, and opinion pieces, and write in response to passages.

Persuasive and Narrative Writing Workbooks
Guided workbooks teach all the skills needed to write narratives and opinion pieces.

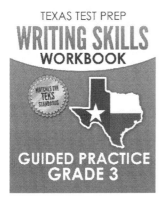 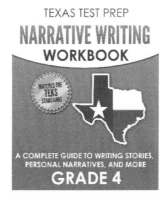 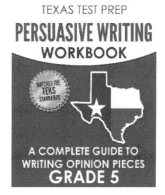

Language

Language Quiz Books
Focused quizzes cover spelling, grammar, writing conventions, and vocabulary.

Revising and Editing Workbooks
Students improve language and writing skills by identifying and correcting errors.

Language Skills Workbooks
Exercises on specific language skills including idioms, synonyms, and homophones.

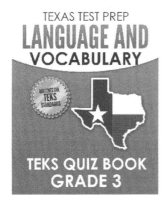  

http://www.testmasterpress.com

Made in the USA
Coppell, TX
30 October 2019